A Simplicity of Faith

JOURNEYS IN FAITH

A Simplicity of Faith
my experience in mourning

William Stringfellow

Journeys in Faith
Robert A. Raines, Editor

ABINGDON
Nashville

A SIMPLICITY OF FAITH:
My Experience in Mourning

Copyright © 1982 by Abingdon

Library of Congress Cataloging in Publication Data

STRINGFELLOW, WILLIAM.
A simplicity of faith.
(Journeys in faith)
1. Bereavement. 2. Grief. 3. Towne, Anthony.
4. Stringfellow, William. I. Title. II. Series.
BV4905.2.S77   248.8'6   81-20625   AACR2

ISBN 0-687-38505-9

"Dead of Winter" (p. 24) reprinted by permission; © 1962 The New Yorker
Magazine, Inc.

"Alpha" (p. 53), "Endscape" (p. 81), and "Poem" (p. 143) are reprinted by
permission; © 1977 the *Anglican Theological Review*.

"End Time" (p. 114) reprinted by permission. © 1979 The Block Island
Writers' Workshop.

The material on page 134, paragraph 2, through page 137, paragraph 2, is
taken with minor adaptations from William Stringfellow, " The Acts of the
Apostles (Continued)," © 1981, Christian Century Foundation. Reprinted by
permission from the April 1, 1981 issue of *The Christian Century*.

Scripture quotations are from The New English Bible, © the Delegates of the
Oxford University Press and the Syndics of the Cambridge University Press
1961, 1970. Reprinted by permission.

MANUFACTURED BY THE PARTHENON PRESS AT
NASHVILLE, TENNESSEE, UNITED STATES OF AMERICA

Acknowledgments

Grateful acknowledgment is made for the assistance of Nancy Greenaway in the preparation of this manuscript.

Some of the material in this book has appeared in other forms in *The Witness* and in *The Christian Century,* and some of it was utilized in lectures at Kirkridge.

By the same author

Conscience & Obedience: The Politics of Romans 13 and Revelation 13 in Light of the Second Coming

An Ethic for Christians and Other Aliens in a Strange Land

A Second Birthday

My People Is the Enemy

Dissenter in a Great Society

Count It All Joy

Free in Obedience

Instead of Death

A Private and Public Faith

As co-author, with Anthony Towne

The Death and Life of Bishop Pike

Suspect Tenderness

The Bishop Pike Affair

for
Bill Kellermann

Contents

Editor's Foreword

People inside and outside the church today are engaged in a profound revisioning of the faith journey. Wanting to honor our own heritage and to be nourished by our roots, we also want to discern the signs of the kingdom now, and to move into the 1980s with a lean biblical, ecumenical, and human faith perspective.

The Journeys in Faith series is offered to facilitate this revisioning of faith. Reflecting on the social justice quest of the 1960s and the inward searching of the 1970s, these books articulate a fresh integration of the faith journey for the years ahead. They are personal and social. Authors have been invited to share what has been happening to them in their faith and life in recent years, and then to focus on issues that have become important for them during this time.

We believe that these lucidly written books will be widely used by study groups in congregations, seminaries, colleges, renewal centers, orders, and denominations, as well as being used for personal study and reflection.

Our distinguished authors embody a diversity of experience and perspective that will provide many points of identification and enrichment for readers. As we enter into the pilgrimages shared in these books, we will find resonance, encouragement and insight for a fresh appropriation of our faith, toward personal and social transformation.

William Stringfellow takes us with him through the valley of the shadow of death of his dear friend and colleague Anthony Towne. "I realized that Anthony's death raised the matter of my vocation once more, in an abrupt, radical, awful, perchance final way." Stringfellow understands *vocation* to be the name for the discernment of the coincidence of the Word of God in history with one's own selfhood. The preface "Biography as Theology" articulates the intention for all the books in this series: that the sharing of one person's faith journey in the context of the Incarnation sheds light for fellow pilgrims on their own faith journeys. So it does in this book.

As Stringfellow grieves and mourns the death of his friend, readers may find themselves, as in a reprise, grieving and mourning once more for losses suffered in their own encounters with death. His acerbic and often droll assessments of doctors, lawyers, and clergy, while costly to those professionals, are priceless to readers. We are required to reappraise our own vocations once more.

Block Island provides the geographical center and spiritual context of this story. It is no coincidence that it is an island, separated from the mainland, but preoccupied with the judgment and salvation of the mainland. Readers are led to ponder the significance of place in their own faith journeys.

One notices the observance of daily liturgy in this story, the practice of two or three gathering in Christ's name, a living house church on Block Island. "Has God abandoned the Church?" asks Stringfellow. Stringfellow has not, tenaciously carrying on his decades-long lover's quarrel with the Church.

The architecture of the book delights the mind's

pleasure in order, even as its four movements bear us along like a musical composition. The author writes with his customary economy and precision, saying just what he means; no more, no less. There is a Spartan character to the book that reflects its author. Stringfellow embodies a simplicity of faith that is on the far side of complexity. Undistracted by sentimentalities, he writes with a passion that offends as it exposes pious and political facsimiles of the truth with which he is obsessed. There are beautiful moments of loving kindness. Such ancient faith-words as *resurrection, conversion, communion of saints,* and *vocation* are sculpted and honed, yielding fresh revelation. As he carves a deep and clear pathway integrating a private and public faith, the essential William Stringfellow becomes visible and audible.

Some readers may remember, when a spouse or dear friend dies in time to come, to read this book again for comfort and courage on the faith journey of grieving and mourning. Some may come back to it when Death, in one of his guises, drives his axe to the root of the question of one's vocation.

Robert A. Raines

Keep me, O God, for in thee have I found refuge.
I have said to the Lord,
'Thou, Lord, art my felicity.'
The gods whom earth holds sacred are all worthless,
and cursed are all who make them their delight;
those who run after them find trouble without end.
I will not offer them libations of blood
nor take their names upon my lips.

Psalm 16:1-4

Preface

Biography as Theology

Winter is the season when Block Island reverts, most nearly, to its original estate. Its winter ambiance is sparse and austere, and there is an impression of purity about it. This is the Island in something resembling its natural condition, unblemished by development, uncluttered by waste, undefiled by crowds. The fixtures and façades of the resort trade are boarded up and abandoned and seem to recede into the landscape. Time is estopped—its domination of existence and activity preempted by weather. The few inhabitants—like the indigenous wildlife—become preoccupied with elementary issues of survival: obtaining food, keeping warm, securing shelter. In the circumstances, though I do not think people love one another any more, they do become more obviously dependent upon each other and are more inclined to help one another in practical ways. In winter, Block Island becomes a basic community.

Paradoxically, winter is often referred to as the "off-season." The contrast is, of course, with *the* season, the summertime, when the cottage folk come and the boat people appear and the ferry "day-trippers" invade; then the shops re-open, the restaurants and bars thrive, and assorted diversions and entertainments flourish. The discrepancy between the Island's ecology and the environment extemporized to convenience the summer

commerce increases each year (or so it seems to me), and
that renders emphatic the truth that the winter is more
definitively *the season,* while the summer is a distortion of
Block Island: an exploitation approaching plunder, an
indulgence breaching squander, a hectic intrusion,
something like rape.

In the period since Anthony Towne and I had
immigrated to Block Island in 1967 (in consequence of
the desperate state of my health, about which I have
written in *A Second Birthday*) both of us had come to
prefer winter rather than summer. (The other two
seasons, which are pleasant enough on the Island, we
considered transitional.) We sometimes talked of quit-
ting the Island during the summer, but we never found
any place to go where summer would not be similarly
commercialized and routined and, more than likely, on a
scale and with a concentration much greater than on
Block Island. Anyway, we found the silence and solitude
of the Island's wintertime to be congenial to our
temperaments and conducive to our vocations. Freed of
superfluity or distraction, on the Island in the winter
Anthony would be a poet, and I a theologian, and each of
us would write, respectively, poetry and theology; and, in
so doing, be who we had been, respectively, called in the
Word of God to be.

Thus, I had set aside the winter of 1979-1980 (apart
from one or two visits to the mainland to make lectures)
to write. There were two manuscripts on my agenda: one
was the completion of the last volume of a trilogy in
theological ethics, a book about the biblical relationship
of the charismatic and the demonic. (The other two
books of the trilogy are *An Ethic for Christians and Other
Aliens in a Strange Land* and *Conscience and Obedience: The
Politics of Romans 13 and Revelation 13 in Light of the Second
Coming.*) The other effort was to contribute a volume to a

series commissioned by Abingdon Press; that is to say, what has since become this book.

I had been having troubles with the trilogy book, occasioned, I recall remarking to Anthony several times, by persistent disruptions in the work attributable to the demonic powers. "They're determined to suppress this book!" I told him. The comment was only semi-facetious, since I am aware, as was Anthony, that exposure is disabling to the demonic (cf. Mark 3:11-30; Luke 11:14-23). They are alert to every effort at identification and apprehensive toward any attempt at elucidation. In any event, I had been plagued once again during these months by health problems. The creative, if radical, surgery that had helped to spare my life in 1968 had simultaneously rendered me diabetic, and now I was suffering some of the complications common to prolonged and advanced diabetes. The circulation in my legs had become so impaired that amputation had become a serious threat, while, at the same time, I was being warned that I would lose my sight gradually within the next few years because of diabetic damage to the blood vessels in my eyes. I was already experiencing intermittent difficulty reading. Meanwhile, I was told, I risked sudden blinding hemorrhage at any time, which might be precipitated by casual effort—such as getting out of bed or bending to tie a shoelace. The problem with my legs was being treated chemically and being monitored on a regular basis in the hope that the condition would not become any more dangerous; laser therapy for my eyes had been recommended by three different medical specialists. The latter involves aiming laser beams into the eyes at the ruptured blood vessels in order to cauterize the hemorrhaged regions and arrest the damage. Anthony was very skeptical about this procedure, since the therapy seemed to be at least as perilous as the ailment. I had agreed, with multifarious qualms, to submit to it because I had been informed that there was no alternative to the procedure.

Despite (perchance because of) the benefit surgery has heretofore been in my life, I do not share the general popular American overconfidence in medical technology. I regard such, anyway, as the most primitive, rather than the most sophisticated, aspect of medical practice. The premise, so prominent in commercialized medicine, that there exists any merely mechanistic remedy for any health problem is, to me, essentially incoherent, categorically false, and usually superstitious. So both Anthony and I were disquieted about the prospect of the laser treatments, and about any possibility of amputation, as much as either of us was concerned about the difficulties I had been having with my eyes and with my legs. In the context of our private communication, my remarks attributing these circumstances and interference with my writing to demonic capabilities was, as I say, only semi-facetious.

Still, I persevered. I felt a very strong conviction about the trilogy book, and I knew that book already, in spite of disruptions in transposing it from my mind into manuscript. The Abingdon book, on the other hand, at that point, was vague to me. My working scheme was to utilize some lectures I was scheduled to give in Canada, in late January, 1980, to focus upon that assignment. I hoped that there would be enough stimulant in the reception of the lectures to enable me to design a book that had substance and integrity. The commission I had received from the publisher was itself indefinite or ambiguous, it seemed to me. I recall the Abingdon correspondence mentioned that several authors were being asked to write about their experience in "revisioning" the faith. I didn't know what that meant. "How can I 'revision' the faith," I asked Anthony one day, as I made some preparations for the Canadian journey, "when I haven't 'visioned' it in the first place?" He never did respond to my query. Then, one week later, Anthony died.

The Canadian trip was aborted. The effort on both books was put aside. The event of Anthony's death overshadowed everything else. At his requiem, celebrated in the dead of winter on Block Island, I understood that I had to face a decision concerning how to expend the remainder of my own life. I decided then to decide nothing suddenly.

Anthony died at 11:28 P.M. on January 28, 1980. By now, as you can read, I have written this book for Abingdon. (The trilogy book is in its final throes.) Whether or not this book represents a "revisioning" of faith, I do not know, because I never got around to learning what that phrase might mean. To my mind, however, *A Simplicity of Faith* represents a sampler of autobiography and biography as theology. More specifically, it tells of my experiences in mourning Anthony's death. It is autobiographical—a book of the same genre as *My People Is the Enemy* and *A Second Birthday*—and, simultaneously, it recounts episodes in the biography of Anthony Towne. Both the autobiographical and biographical aspects become, and are, the data for the theological reflection and commentary of the book.

I consider the theological treatment of biography—and, more broadly, history—to be biblically apropos; after all, the Old Testament is, to a large extent, Israel's story, just as the Gospel accounts tell the story of Jesus and his disciples, while the Book of the Acts is biography of the apostles and the other pioneer Christians who became the Apostolic Church. Similar affirmations can be made of the Epistles, and, for that matter, the prisoner's diary which is the Book of Revelation.

The theological exploration of biography or the theological reconnaisance of history are apt, and even normative, styles because each is congruent with the definitive New Testament insight and instruction: *the Incarnation*. Biblical faith is distinguished from all religions, all philosophies, and all ideologies by its redundant insistence upon the presence and vitality of the Word of God in common history; and Christians particularly confess that the involvement of the Word of God in the life of this world becomes most conscientious, comprehensible, and intentional in the event of Jesus Christ. This historic, incarnate activity of the Word of God signifies the militance of the Word of God, both in cosmic dimensions of space and time and in each and every item of created life, including *your* personhood and *your* biography or mine. It is this same basis of the Christian faith that is so often diminished, dismissed, omitted, or ignored when theology is rendered in abstract, hypothesized, propositional or academic models. There is, then, with the latter something incongruent about the mode of theological discourse— something inherently inappropriate about the method being employed to present the gospel. So, I believe, biography (and history), *any* biography and *every* biography, is inherently theological, in the sense that it contains already—literally by virtue of the Incarnation—the news of the gospel whether or not anyone discerns that. *We* are each one of us parables.

What I am referring to here amounts, of course, to a doctrine of revelation. What I am discussing is how the living Word of God is implicated in the actual life of this world, in all its tumult and excitement, ambiguity and change, in the existence of the nations and principalities, human beings and other creatures, in every happening in every place in every moment (cf. Revelation 19:11-16). This world is the scene where the Word of God is; fallen creation—in all of its scope, detail, and diversity—is the milieu in which the Word of God is disclosed and apprehended; Jesus Christ verifies how the Word of God may be beheld by those who have sight and hearing to notice and give heed to the Word of God (cf. John 1:1-14).

Biography, thus, is rudimentary data for theology, and every biography is significant for the knowledge it yields of the Word of God incarnate in common life, whether or not the subject of the biography is aware of that significance of his or her own story. *Vocation* is the name of the awareness of *that* significance of one's own biography. To have a vocation or to be called in Christ means to discern the coincidence of the Word of God with one's own selfhood, in one's own being, in its most specific, thorough, unique, and conscientious sense.

I had confronted the vocational issue earlier in my own biography—in my work in the East Harlem ghetto, in the experience of profound illness, in the immigration, with Anthony, to Block Island. Thence, in the midst of the requiem for Anthony, I realized that Anthony's death raised the matter of my vocation once more, in an abrupt, radical, awful, perchance final, way. That is the topic of this book.

I do not anticipate that either my grief at Anthony's death or my mourning for Anthony's life will be exhausted or concluded by the writing of this book. The fact that I have been able to write it only indicates that both my grieving and my mourning have matured enough—beyond initial traumas—to become continuing features of my daily life. I do not expect the grief to ever be fully dissipated; I do not want the mourning to ever be completed. Furthermore, I think that, in the months that have elapsed since 11:28 P.M. on January 28, 1980, I have grieved and mourned sufficiently so that I now distinguish the one from the other. I mention that here, at the outset of this book, because it informs and affects everything else I have written in this book.

I understand grief to be the total experience of loss, anger, outrage, fear, regret, melancholy, abandonment, temptation, bereftness, helplessness suffered privately, within one's self, in response to the happening of death. By distinction and contrast, I comprehend mourning as the liturgies of recollection, memorial, affection, honor, gratitude, confession, empathy, intercession, meditation, anticipation for the life of the one who is dead. Empirically, in the reality of someone's death, and in the aftermath of it, grief and mourning are, of course, jumbled. It is, I think, part of the healing of mourning to sort out and identify the one from the other. In any case, of all those I have known and loved and grieved and mourned, Anthony's life was the closest to my own, and the most complementary, so his death is my most intimate experience in grief and mourning. From that experience—so far—what I have to say is: grieving is about weeping and wailing and gnashing of teeth; mourning is about rejoicing—rejoicing in the Lord. From that standpoint, I confess I have found mourning Anthony an exquisite, bittersweet experience. I *enjoy* mourning Anthony.

Such sentiments would not surprise Anthony. Sometimes he accused me of being stoic. The doctors constantly report that I have a very high tolerance of pain. (I usually tell them that is a matter of their luck, not mine.) I prefer to consider myself very patient. Whatever the appropriate way to put it, there was a difference between Anthony and me in this respect. He was impatient, intolerant of pain, not given to stoicism. He was quickly outraged by injustice; he complained promptly of suffering—whether his own or others'. He was indignant toward death. He spent much effort prompting and prodding me when I would be tempted to procrastinate or rationalize. (He attributed these temptations to the odd circumstance that I was trained as a lawyer but became a theologian. He considered the poet's art more humanized than either law or theology.)

After the requiem on Block Island, Scott Kennedy, who had come from California, for himself and on behalf of other friends there, remained with me for several days. There are few other people I would have been glad to have with me in the household at that time. Scott, who is the brother-in-law of the late Bishop James A. Pike, about whom Anthony and I had written two books, is a good friend and compatriot, and he and I talked in those days—as one would expect—about Anthony's life and its meaning for each of us. At one point in our dialogue, Scott asked me directly what, above or beyond everything else, Anthony had meant to me.

"Anthony is my conscience," I confided in Scott.

It was an instantaneous and spontaneous reply. And the response was no hyperbole, least of all in the circumstances. It is unembellished, and it needs no embellishment.

That is my epithet for Anthony Towne.

William Stringfellow

Lent, 1981
Eschaton
Block Island, Rhode Island

DEAD OF WINTER

The city shuffles through the snow, the whirling snow, and I, indifferent
To cold, remember how he looked, the casket much too small, the grief a
Discomfort buried under triumphs of survival—memories
Of snowdrifts hollowed out, as I am hollowed out, a snowman
Dissolving into frozen sunlight, caving into dust,
A drift of words, iambic flights of migratory
Goodbyes, a dead-of-winter funeral, the earth
Too stiff to weep, the open grave a trenchant
Disclosure. Nothing lasts and nothing lives
Forever; even now the city
Disintegrates in gusts of snow,
The words revolve like poems
Around a solitude
Of empty feelings,
Around myself,
Until, dead,
Alone,
I,
Alive,
Begin to
Feel tears run down
My face, the plowed-up
Drifts melting into slush.
An alley cat, emerging,
Shakes off paralysis, accepts
The warm, triumphant sun; the pigeons,
A flock in flight, discover crusts of bread
Among old ladies blinking through the park, as
Regrets give way to tremblings underground, murmurings,
And I, delivered from despair, rejoice, remember
How, snowbound, schools were closed, toboggans hurtled down the street
A snowball slowly rolled across the yard became a beach ball—
Bright colors spinning into golden suns, reflective moons, as words
That whirl become a warm embrace, a dance of birds across an open
Astonishment of sky, and I, I think of you, I think that you know why.

—ANTHONY TOWNE

I

Dread

Anthony's death was a shock—a momentous shock—to me, but at the same time, in a curious way, it was no surprise.

a touch of "flu"

It happened in a single day. On Monday, the 28th of January, 1980, he suddenly became desperately ill, was taken by the Block Island Rescue Squad to the nearest mainland hospital, in Westerly, Rhode Island, lingered for some hours and died. The only forewarning of his death, if it be that, had come a few days earlier, on Wednesday of the previous week, when Anthony complained at breakfast that he felt tired and supposed he might have the flu. He decided to return to bed to rest. He opposed calling the town physician: he had little confidence in the medical profession anyway, regarding most doctors as parasitical. His attitude was, in part, influenced by my experiences in illness, but only partly so. There had been some other episode, an earlier experience of his own that he never fully related to me, which had originated his suspicious conviction. So he remained in bed for a few days nursing himself—he drank lots of juices and took a few aspirins, snoozed and read. He had a slight fever, fatigue, a diminished appetite, but there seemed to be no cause for alarm. He assumed as I did, that he had influenza. It was epidemic in the region then, as it commonly is in January in New England.

I had for a long time been booked to go to London, Ontario, to give some lectures at the University of Western Ontario and at certain of the neighboring seminaries during the week beginning January 27. On that morning Anthony arose and had a normal breakfast at table with me. His temperature had virtually returned to normal. His morale seemed good and he said he felt much improved and considered that the "flu" would pass in another day or two. I raised the question of deferring the Canadian trip, but he was insistent that I undertake it, as scheduled. I accepted his judgment on the matter, but asked a neighbor to visit the house each day during my absence to see that Anthony was all right and to care for his meals and other needs. The neighbor, Nancy Greenaway, came over on that Sunday afternoon and discussed these arrangements with both Anthony and myself. Later that day I departed for Ontario.

My trip to London was unremarkable—in fact, it was boring. As soon as possible after my arrival, I retired. I slept very fitfully, a rare circumstance for me, but something I attributed to the adjustments of travel. I rose at sunrise, as I do every day, prayed, worked some on the lectures to be given, injected my flank with insulin, dressed, and took a walk, found a newspaper, had breakfast, and waited for the rest of the world to wake up. Around nine o'clock I telephoned Block Island. Nancy answered the call and told me that everything at *Eschaton* (the name of our household) seemed fine, and that Anthony was still sleeping. I said that I would phone again later in the day. Some minutes before I was supposed to deliver the first of the lectures, at a luncheon for faculty and chaplains at the university, I received an urgent message to telephone the Island. This time Mary Donnelly, the resident nurse on the Island, told me that Anthony had very suddenly become "disoriented," that she had been summoned and had found indications that he was bleeding internally, so that the Rescue Squad had been called to take Anthony to Westerly Hospital. Mary considered that Anthony's condition was extremely grave and advised me to return quickly.

Airline connections between London, Ontario, and Westerly, Rhode Island, are not frequent or convenient; and I ascertained that I could depart from London no sooner than about four o'clock that afternoon to connect through Kennedy Airport to Providence. I arranged for the Island air taxi service to meet that flight and take me on to Westerly. This way I could reach Westerly about ten that night. I told my hosts the news, went ahead and delivered that initial lecture—it seemed preferable to just loitering around—and spent some time alone to think and pray, and boarded the airplane.

My recollection of the trip to the hospital is a blur of surrealistic sights and impressions in which I cannot sharply distinguish between what was happening in my mind—flooded, as it was now, by the recall of everything that Anthony and I had ever shared in our common life—and what was otherwise happening as I went through the routines of travel—changing tickets, submitting to airport "security" screenings, being processed through customs, hustling to make connections between planes. I have traveled enough to become conditioned to endure such procedures numbly, though I resent them as indignities, and that experience sustained me, in a practical way, on this somber journey.

I managed to make calls to the hospital three times while en route and learned that Anthony was in intensive care. Each report of his condition was more ominous than the one before. I tried, also, to reach Anthony's mother, Margaret Towne, at her home in Haverhill, Massachusetts, but none of my phone calls were completed to her. Between planes in Toronto I bought some candy and some orange juice in order to deliberately increase my blood-sugar count and thereby spare myself an insulin shock occasioned by the stress of the trip. Meanwhile, most of the time, my attention was elsewhere, preoccupied in the recall of our friendship. At times, I used the *Book of Common Prayer* to ratify my endeavor in Anthony's behalf.

deathwatch

The air taxi from the Island met the flight in Providence and took me to Westerly, where a cab was waiting to drive me to the hospital. I arrived at the intensive care unit shortly after ten o'clock. Somehow word had reached Anthony's mother and she had driven to the hospital and had reached Anthony's bedside only minutes before my own arrival. Nancy Greenaway was there—she, thoughtfully, provided me with some orange juice—and Father David Joslin, the Rector of Christ Church, Westerly, who also served the congregation of St. Ann's mission on Block Island, to which Anthony and I had been connected. The doctor on duty told me there was no hope that Anthony would survive.

I spent some time alone with Anthony. His body had been fitted with an array of medical contraptions. He would not have wanted that, had he the choice. I remembered his vigil when I had been in similar distress and how Bishop Pike had joined him there and unction had been given to me. I touched Anthony's brow, making the sign of the Cross. I let my tears anoint him. His eyes saw me and in a faint sound he greeted me. Then he sighed, exhausted.

Bruce Gillie, who is my physician for the treatment of my diabetes, came in. He, principally, had been caring for Anthony all day, and he told me what had happened since Anthony had been admitted to the hospital that morning. The internal bleeding had not been controlled, and the cause of it had not been determined. There had been a steady deterioration, punctuated by the failure of one body system after another. I asked about the contraptions, realizing that Anthony would dislike them, and about any risk that he would linger indefinitely. Anthony's conviction, like my own, opposed any contrived, mechanistic, or artificial maintenance when a person had irretrievably lost the human faculties, so I made it very clear that I would not countenance any such tort against Anthony. When I joined the others in vigil, I mentioned the same issue to Margaret, and she indicated that she respected Anthony's position in the matter.

The precaution was not needed. I again visited the room where Anthony lay. His body stirred, but I do not suppose that he could see anymore. I took a hand of his in one of mine. The only thing I said to him was, "Thank you." I looked at the clock. It was 11:28 P.M.

a familiarity with death

I have mentioned that Anthony's death was an immense shock to me, but that it was, in a sense, no surprise. It was traumatic in every obvious way that the sudden and apparently premature death of a loved one is. Anthony was only fifty-one years old; he was, from all appearances, robust; there had been no forewarning in illness, apart from that touch of "flu"; he had been, I think, at the prime of his gifts as poet; he had transcended the threat of alcoholism that, earlier, had harassed him; he remained an unusually shy and private person, but he no longer was tempted to be a recluse, and indeed, he had in the past few years assumed a significant role in the Block Island community; he was a friend to many, a pastor to some; his life had specific meaning for an astonishing diversity of people, both on the Island and in America (as the mainland is called by Islanders).

The shock for me at his death, for reasons such as these, was accentuated by the fact that, between ourselves, Anthony and I had contemplated that I would be the first to die. That was the common-sense expectation ever since what Anthony sometimes referred to as my "famous illness," simply because the conditions of my living were so precarious, so complicated, so delicate. Both of us had been required by the peculiar circumstances of my health to consider the prospect of my death, and so, to that extent, each of us was prepared for it. As I say, it was taken for granted between us that I would likely die before Anthony did.

Be that as it may, I was aware that Anthony would prefer, if we did not die in a common disaster, to be the first to die, and, as the *Book of Common Prayer* puts it, "depart hence in the Lord."

That is one reason that his death, albeit traumatic, was not a surprise. Death was a familiar reference in our household, and there is little, I think that death can do that would astonish either Anthony or myself. By death, in this context, I mean something more than death deemed a destination, or something different from death in its vulgar funereal connotations; by death, here, I name the (paradoxically) *living* moral reality of death present in this history, pervasive in every aspect of the existence of this world, insinuating ultimate significance, and, therefore, claiming imminent consequence for human life and for the life of the whole of Creation.

Death, so construed and so apprehended, is a redundant biblical topic, and, for that reason, it was a frequent reference in the dialogue of the community of Anthony and myself. We were constantly discussing death—in its multifarious manifestations, public and personal. The same subject recurs frequently in Anthony's poetry and prose, as it does in my writing about theology and ethics.

I do not imply that death was a morbid fascination for either of us, but rather that both of us shared the belief that all of history—and all particular experience within history—consists of the drama and the dialectic of death and resurrection. Artistically authentic poetry exposes that drama; biblically authentic theology elucidates that dialectic. Well, we each took death very seriously as death deserves, and that was evident, in many different ways, in our common life. Anthony always read all the obituaries in the *New York Times* every day. He would brief me about these reports and, when it seemed appropriate or necessary, names would be mentioned and people remembered in the intercessions we customarily shared at mealtime.

Among many other episodes that had formed our convictions and attitudes toward death was, of course, my "famous illness," but that was hardly the only one. There was as well our long and close involvement with Bishop Pike eventuating, some time after his death, in the biography, *The Death and Life of Bishop Pike*. The juxtaposition in the title of *Death* and *Life* is very deliberate in order to indicate the manner in which the death of Pike was foreshadowed in his life, or, to put the same idea differently, to show that the story of his life was simultaneously the story of his dying; but then, furthermore, to affirm in the construction of the title that resurrection succeeds death. The issues that, in Anthony's life, occasioned the threat of alcoholism had also much to do with the militancy of death, and these became part of our shared effort to comprehend death and to avail ourselves of the Word of God, which has broken the reign of death in this world.

And, as would be expected, very prominent in our common experience was that of our being the "Block Island Two"—as Eugene McCarthy had styled us—indicted by the regime of Richard Nixon and John Mitchell and J. Edgar Hoover for harboring Daniel Berrigan, the fugitive priest. That was how we learned, firsthand, of the chill of death incarnated politically in the perversion of the legal process. We realized at the same time, in 1970 and 1971, that the target of that assault was our humanity—the very *esse* of our humanness: sanity and conscience—and we struggled hard not to succumb to paranoia while we were under ubiquitous surveillance and relentless harassment. We often laughed, later on, when the truth—or some of it—about the Nixon-Mitchell-Hoover cabal began to be exposed and it turned out that their schemes far, far exceeded our worst imaginations. Realistically, our endangerment was actually much greater than our fear, and what we called our paranoia was virtually complacency, so portentous was the effort mounted during the Nixon reign to neutralize the constitutional inheritance and subvert due process of law. Whatever our naïveté, in the circumstances, at the time, we were able to recognize that the Nixon administration quite literally stank of death and embodied the idolatry of death as its operative morality.

In these and in innumerable other ways, Anthony and I had become well acquainted with the power of death in the life of this world. In that sense, we were different in our routine of life from those, say, who presuppose in their lifestyle that death is somehow remote from history or merely a destination or a biological condition, or from those who, incredibly, pretend that death does not exist.

In such a context, Anthony's death came as no surprise to me.

a premonition of death?

When anyone dies, those who remain who love the dead person are apt to have a plethora of queries to which no answers are known or can be known until the very Day of Judgment. Either the answers are secreted with the dead or they are otherwise beyond the reach of the bereaved. I notice that many people, in grief, indulge such questions, become obsessed by them, sometimes unnecessarily suffer guilt because of them.

In the event of Anthony's death, virtually all questions related to the proximate cause of his death remain unanswered. Within moments of his death, the attending doctors urged that an autopsy be done, and that was authorized and performed, but the medical examiner's report ascribes his death to internal bleeding without going further to identify the cause of that bleeding. The only thing the autopsy confirms is that the coroner was satisfied that it was a death due to so-called natural causes. Some friends, at the time, urged that I protest the superficiality of the typically bureaucratic autopsy report that had been rendered, but I considered that this would be dissipation for me without, at the same time, yielding any hint of benefit to Anthony, to Anthony's memory, to Anthony's relatives or friends. Besides, there were other queries that preoccupied my attention.

On the morning after Anthony's death, after I had returned to the Island and had had some time at *Eschaton* alone, I went to the Manger, a small out-building separate from the house, which had been Anthony's study. We called it "the Manger" because it had been originally built as a stable for a horse that the previous owners of the property had kept. (The building enjoyed brief notoriety in 1970, because it is where Daniel Berrigan stayed while the FBI was trying to find him. The *Providence Journal-Bulletin* heralded Dan's capture with a banner headline: HE HID IN 'THE MANGER'.) Despite that, the Manger was a most private domain. Apart from Dan, there had never been any other guest there. I seldom went there or disturbed Anthony while he was there. It was his space, his monastic closet, really; it is where he worked on his poetry and at his correspondence; it is where he planned his gardens, and where he considered how best to care for the birds in the winter; it is where he read—voluminously; it is where he prayed in a formal and self-conscious sense. Every morning, early, after we had had breakfast and heard the news reports, Anthony would raise a flag—sometimes several, according to the season and happenings to be observed, and then go out to the Manger where, first of all, he kept the daily offices according to the *Book of Common Prayer*. Raising a flag, of course, can be an intercession, too, and it usually was in our household. But in addition to that, and besides our spontaneous meditations at mealtimes, Anthony faithfully recited the daily offices. Then he usually would spend the rest of the morning writing.

I thought of his accustomed routine when I walked out to the Manger that morning after Anthony had died, and, not unexpectedly, discovered the prayerbook open, face up, in the middle of his desk, as he had left it. Nearby on the desktop there was a neat pile of papers and a small typewriter. Anthony's desk had been so positioned in the room, adjacent to a large picture window, that when sitting at it one commanded a marvelous view of the cliffs and the ocean and (Anthony sometimes remarked)

Portugal, our nearest neighbor in the east. I sat down, and only then looked at the page to which the prayerbook was opened. It was a page whereon there is a prayer often used by a sick person for his or her own health and faith. I knew that during those few days Anthony had spent in bed with the so-called flu, he had, despite the severe weather, gone out to the Manger at least once. I had scolded him for doing so dressed only in a bathrobe and a great fuzzy scarf. Was that when he had made this prayer? Perchance, I wondered, he had suffered some premonition that his "flu" was more than he had admitted to me.

My eyes wandered further over the desktop. The stack of papers was secured by a stone that I recognized as one of those we had gathered at Masada, when we had visited Israel after the death there of Bishop Pike, while working together on the Pike biography. It was not a casual souvenir, not only because of its connection in our minds with Jim Pike, but also because we had both been so impressed and moved at Masada and by the witness of the Jews, *our* ancestors, against tyrannical rule that had held sway there long ago. This was where the Jews had determined to die, by their own effort, rather than submit to imperious aggression and lawless authority. This was where, as Josephus has reported, a decision to die had meant a commitment to freedom for human life, an ultimate act of conscience. Anthony and I had both been awed and fascinated in our pilgrimage to Masada, and Anthony's paperweight was a rock he had picked up there and carried all the way back to Block Island.

I lifted the Masada stone and examined the papers it had been keeping neatly. On top was a three-page typed piece. It was in the style and scheme of a newspaper item and bore this headline:

AGED POET DEAD ON BLOCK ISLAND

END OF AN ERA

DEATH ATTRIBUTED TO EXHAUSTION

I realized that Anthony had written his own obituary. Premonition, indeed.

the obituary of God

I looked up from reading Anthony's obituary to a place on one of the walls of the Manger where there hung a framed copy of the "obituary of God," which Anthony had composed in 1966. The style Anthony's had been written in instantly reminded me of the earlier obituary. That had become a very celebrated piece, eventually translated into more than thirty languages and reprinted throughout the world, as befitted the subject.

The obituary of God was written at the climax of the so-called death of God movement. Anthony had been reading that literature and found it trivial, pretentious, and literally profane. One evening he wrote the obituary of God as a satirical commentary on the "death of God movement." When he had finished it, he summoned me to the study, in the apartment we then shared on West Seventy-ninth Street in Manhattan, and read it aloud, in much the same manner as he habitually read other noteworthy obituaries to me.

It was written out of his own exasperation with this theological vogue, and for our private entertainment; he had no intention of publishing it. Anthony seldom made any effort to publish what he wrote, and he virtually never wrote with publication as a motivation. He wrote as art. He was very wary that the conditions requisite for publishing in America intimidate or compromise the art.

To write for money was, to him, essentially incongruous. So most of what he wrote has not been published, as yet, and what he wrote that has been published, has been so at the behest of others.

It seemed to me the obituary of God was too pertinent and too delightful to not be shared, by not being published, and so I caused a copy of it to reach the *New York Times*. Since it was written in the syntax of a *Times* obituary, it was, I suppose, a ridicule of the *Times*, as well as of the death of God movement. The *Times* did not promptly publish it. A few days after it was written, however, B. J. Stiles, then editor of *motive* magazine, which has since—lamentably—been suppressed by the ecclesiastical bureaucrats of the Methodist Church hierarchy, was our dinner guest. In the course of the evening, Anthony shared the obituary with B. J. He appreciated it immensely and he immediately asked to publish it in *motive*. It appeared there in the February, 1966, issue, in a format and typeface identical to that used in the *Times*.

The piece enjoyed prompt and prolonged notoriety from its publication in *motive* and, at the crest of that response, the *New York Sunday Times*, in its "News of the Week" section, reprinted the item as it had first appeared in *motive*. It was then, too, that Harper & Row commissioned Anthony to write a satirical book in the same realm, which Anthony agreed, warily, to do. The result was the book, *Excerpts from the Diaries of the Late God*.

Anthony's practical indifference to publishing, and his concern about the difficulties of keeping creative integrity in the prevailing circumstances of the American publishing system, seemed to him fully justified when the *Excerpts* was finished and he endured repeated editorial harassments about the manuscript, chiefly from hucksters, such as those who have so heavily infiltrated the publishing trade, many of them no more than semiliterate and disinterested in ideas, but who are much preoccupied with merchandising techniks.

Block Island, later on, was to provide an ambiance in which Anthony could write as an artistic and, in truth, charismatic endeavor—and not as a commercial venture—especially so by the time the Writers Workshop there was organized. I told Nancy Greenaway, a colleague of Anthony's in the workshop, about the obituary I had discovered in the Manger. She brought to me another piece, a brief autobiography entitled "The Story of Anthony Towne by Anthony Towne," which he had written a few months earlier when each member of the workshop had agreed to write his or her own biography.

Since responsibility for the requiem was mine, I decided that, as eulogy, the obituary and the autobiography, together with a poem or two of Anthony's should be read by some of his fellow writers from the workshop. Thus, in death, Anthony would speak for himself.

a discretion in dying

I do not know whether Anthony experienced any specific premonition of his death during those days next before he died. In a broader significance, I do believe that in his death he retained a discretion about dying. By that I mean that, though he was relatively young in years, in his maturity as a human being he was ready to die. His death happened quickly and was unpredictable, but he had been prepared to die for some time prior to his death so that his death was not frantic. There was, so far as I can affirm, no important aspect of his being left secreted, suppressed, omitted, or otherwise unfulfilled. One is not indifferent to the particular circumstances of his dying, but all that is incidental to the truth of his death. His dying—and when and where and how he died—did not abort his life. His death did not frustrate the gift he understood life to be. He was composed. Anthony was morally capable of accepting his own death, and, when he died, he had already accepted his death. He was reconciled within himself and with the rest of Creation in the Word of God. Paradoxically, it is when a human being can be said to be most authentically alive that that person becomes free to die imminently or at any moment. I can testify that Anthony knew and enjoyed that freedom.

Theologically speaking, what I am talking about is the meaning of the death in Christ that emancipates a human being from bondage to death. Anthony had, long since, suffered whatever the power of death and the fear or thrall of the power of death could do to him, and, in that suffering, he had encountered the grace of the Word of God enabling him to transcend that suffering. So the threat of death no longer held sway over his life, and dying held no surprise for him, no new knowledge and no novel apprehension. Having already died in Christ, his selfhood had been rescued, established, identified, fulfilled, and finished, so that his death, while poignant, was not waste or tragedy or demonic triumph or incentive to despair. In traditional syntax, Anthony had found his life in his loss of life in Christ.

It was a feature of the community that exists between us that Anthony and I could speak openly of such matters as these. And if our dialogue was, as I have previously mentioned, often about death—and its manifold significance—it was just as often about resurrection—and its multifarious implications for this life in this world. We were much aware of how the efficacy of the resurrection for living here and now impinges, among many other ways, upon dying.

For instance, we both knew people who, having the freedom of those who die in Christ, can be said to have actually decided when to die. Our neighbor on Block Island, Katharine Breydert, seemed to us to be such a person. She died only three months before Anthony died, and it was not happenstance that they had become great friends through the years that they had been contemporaries on the Island. Katharine and her husband, Frederick, had come to America as refugees from the Nazis. Frederick is a gifted composer, his career in music disrupted and curtailed by his concentration camp experience. Katharine, somewhat his senior, had been a pioneer woman physician in Austria. She was born a Jew and was converted to the Christian faith and had become a truly devout Roman Catholic. After arriving in this country, Katharine had been able to resume her medical practice and had worked at that for some years in Greenwich Village before moving to Block Island to retire as a doctor. Soon after meeting the Breyderts, Anthony and I discovered that we shared with them many mutual New York friends. Katharine, as one example, had for years been the personal physician of Dorothy Day—until she withdrew because Dorothy was such an obstinate patient: thus they could remain steadfast friends. The bond between the Breyderts and our household deepened especially during the time of our hospitality to Daniel Berrigan, S. J., and in the aftermath of his seizure at *Eschaton* by a crowd of federal agents. Dan's most recent Island visit, prior to Anthony's death, had been to celebrate the requiem at Katharine's death in the Chapel of St. Andrew's parish.

Katharine Breydert was a resolute Christian: pious, but not pietistic; zealous, but patient; fragile, but formidable; long-suffering, but steadfast. She had received abundant gifts, the most remarkable among

them being her gift as a liturgical artist. She had honored
this gift during the Nazi experience, when she was exiled
and separated from Frederick, by making collages of
biblical themes from bits of paper. All of these had been
carefully kept until, on the Island, she and "good
Frederick," as she often called him, painstakingly
executed them in mosaic or stained glass. In the latter
years of her life, Katharine contracted various ailments
and, episodically, seemed so frail that one expected her
to expire momentarily. Medically, her death was
indicated long before it happened. Finally, when she
knew that the translation of her program of collages into
glass and stone would be completed, she decided to die,
and did. It seemed to both Anthony and myself that
dying had become for Katharine a matter of protocol
between Almighty God and Katharine, and, whatever
the attitude of God about it, Katharine would allow no
interference with it until her work, her offertory, really,
was done. As Nurse Mary Donnelly put it once,
"Katharine had made a bargain with the Lord, and she
kept it." So did the Lord.

That view of Katharine's death was exemplified the
night before she died. A few friends had been
summoned to the house, since Katharine was thought to
be dying. Frederick had been playing his own music for
her for some hours. Katharine, lying there, seemed
virtually dead. Suddenly, aware of the cluster of people
nearby, Katharine opened her eyes, looked at us, and
said, quite firmly, "You can all go home. I will listen to
Frederick's music!" Katharine died, peaceably, the
following evening, ready, at last, to meet the Lord.

Another death that arrested our concern was that of
Henry Pitney Van Dusen, retired president of Union
Theological Seminary in New York City, whom I had
known especially in connection with ecumenical involve-

ment in the World Council of Churches and with whom
both Anthony and I had occasional contact in the city.
Van Dusen evinced vigor, strength, and capability,
intellectual and physical, which we each admired, all the
more so because Van Dusen's virtues seemed to us
qualities gradually but noticeably diminishing among
nominal leaders of American Christendom. As in so
many other institutions, a translation has been taking
place in the churches from leadership to management,
and, in the process, imagination, courage, authority—
such as Van Dusen epitomized—are being displaced by
technical proficiency, administrative mediocrity, bureaucratic sophistication, mere routine. Anthony frequently
lamented this. "The great people are dying," he would
say, interrupting his audit of the *Times* obituaries. If
there was a touch of romanticism in such a comment,
there was substantive truth in it too. For John Maury
Allin to sit in the chair of Arthur Lichtenberger, as
presiding bishop of the Episcopal Church, is as
ridiculous as having Richard Milhaus Nixon in the chair
of Franklin Roosevelt as President; and, in both
instances, the substitution represents momentous
change in church and nation.

Anyway, we regarded Van Dusen as one of the great
personages of the times. The circumstances of his death
were more or less suppressed, because he decided, after a
disabling stroke, to end his own life. His wife did the
same, at the same time. From what we could learn these
were acts of, so to say, self-administered euthanasia.
They were distinguishable from Katharine Breydert's
decision to die: she had defied the ordinary limitations of
her health in order to ready her offering; the Van
Dusens had acted to spare their family and friends and
themselves the dehumanizing sufferings of profound
incapacity. They asserted a conclusive right of self-

determination preempting the customary medical and ecclesiastical claims. We regretted exceedingly that Van Dusen's gesture did not generate the public consideration and discussion that it invited and deserved. In our conversations, Anthony and I somehow associated the Van Dusen decision to die with Masada. It certainly did not seem to be a suicide to us. Perhaps, for the Van Dusens, the only way to value their own humanity in life was to die humanly by their own decision and act, instead of as victims of radical disability or as captives of the American health care system.

Since then, of course, there have been other events that evoke echoes of Masada. Consider the deaths, by voluntary starvation, of the IRA prisoners, like Bobby Sands. Notice that the ecclesiastical authorities accorded requiems for Sands and his peers because, it was said, their deaths were deemed sacrifices rather than suicides. Now, remember the Buddhist immolations during the Vietnam War? Must these acts not be considered very similar to the "sacrifices" of the IRA prisoners? Are not both much the same as Masada? In any of these various situations, what sanctifies one but not others?

the idolatry of death

Any questions such as these, articulated in attempts to distinguish between "suicide" and "sacrifice," or between "suicide" and "self-determination," or to make any similar discriminations, are pretentious. All such questions remain true conundrums. They are questions which yield no answers free from the tricks of sophistry. These are questions without general, hypothetical, or abstract answers. They have no answers that are ethically correct or morally right. Any so-called answers to questions of this sort are ethically arbitrary and, usually, simply self-serving.

This is by way of saying that these are issues that have only *historic* answers; that is, the "answers" of actual events and experiences. Masada happened. So did the deaths of the IRA prisoners. Each must be taken seriously as an event, and no ethical or moral inferences can be extracted from one and imposed on the other. Again, such questions have existential "answers": Van Dusen took initiative in his own death. Bobby Sands fasted to death. Some Buddhists ignited their own bodies. Each happening is so radically subjective that it is morally unique. Humanly speaking, there is no way to evaluate what has happened. That assessment literally awaits the prerogative of the Judgment of the Word of God at the consummation of history. As to that Judgment, no person and no principality—least of all the professed church—has insight. The specificity of the Judgment of the Word of God endures as mystery until the end and fulfillment of the era of time. And, as Saint Paul was mindful, every effort to second-guess the Judgment of the Word of God is, for humans or for institutions, a dissipation.

There are other topics wherein similar problems of morality or ethical theory arise; notably and venerably, for example, in connection with the "just war" doctrine so familiar in Western Christendom. Since its origination in the Constantinian ethos of European and, subsequently, American churches—since, in other words, the acquisition by these churches of so radical a vested interest in the preservation of incumbent political regimes, military establishments, and the economic status quo—the teaching has been propagated that warfare can be morally justified if it safeguards a nation's cause against aggression and the threat of tyranny. In fact, of course, the "just war" notion has been proclaimed, notoriously, in simultaneous rationalizations of diametrically opposing powers. In recent history, it has been redundantly asserted by *both* sides in the American Revolution, by *both* sides in the American Civil War, by *both* sides in the First World War, and again, vehemently, by *both* sides in the Second World War. It has been used apologetically in most of the conflicts of manifest destiny and colonial expansion and in most wars of national liberation, as well. It became rudimentary Cold War doctrine in *both* the United States and the Soviet Union and is still recited ritually in that context. It was even invoked at the outset of American adventurism in Vietnam—under the auspices of Cardinal Spellman, among others—until the genocidal reality of that war refuted the credibility of the claim.

Lately, however, when a "just war" rubric has been officially sponsored to rationalize immense escalation and terrific acceleration of nuclear weapons production and deployment, that rubric has begun to be challenged as morally ambiguous. People, despite prolonged conditioning to the contrary, sense that it is *inherently* incoherent to speak of waging a "just war" with nuclear arms capable of exterminating life as it has been known on the planet. (It was, after all, that very same moral ambiguity—the policy of obliterating villages and hamlets in order to "save" them—that was significant in converting public sentiment against the war in Vietnam.)

I would press the logic to its appropriate conclusion: the violence of warfare, whether nuclear or otherwise, is generically incapable of vindicating any cause deemed just. The correlation, theologically speaking, is between the violence of war and the justice of the cause in which *that* violence distorts and destroys *that* justness. Americans ought to have learned that in the Second World War, if not elsewhere, when the military supremacy accomplished by the United States in that effort sponsored a technology and a technocracy incompatible with the American Constitutional system. That outcome of the Second World War to this day defines the parameters of the American political crisis. Reviving the militaristic mentality popularized in that war will hardly cope with that crisis.

In the discourse between Anthony and myself, as that was prompted by various events, the burden of discussion was never focused on moral or ethical assessments of an occurrence. I do not recall that we ever asked such a question as, "Was Van Dusen morally justified in precipitating his own death in the way he did for the reasons he cited?" Judgment belongs to the Word of God. Instead, our attention concentrated upon the issue of idolatry of the power of death, and whether, in the circumstances known to us, the power of death was being upheld as the ultimate moral reality in the life of this world. The question commanding our concern was, thus, whether Van Dusen's decision and action constituted a regard for the power of death as if death held ultimate moral significance in history—as if death were God.

That idolatry is endemic in the nation and its culture in America (though no more than in other societies). In truth it is the condition of the Fall, the very bondage unto death from which the freedom of new life in Christ is vouchsafed. That idolatry is manifest literally in the complicated commerce of war that increasingly dominates the whole of American society, but it takes other forms, some attractive or beguiling. Indeed, even that idolatry evidenced in the nuclear peril is commended to people as the guarantor of "security" and "peace." Meanwhile, General Electric "brings good things to living," we are told, but does the corporation profit more from making cones for nuclear warheads or from marketing refrigerators? How many products of the pharmaceutical industry jeopardize human life but are merchandised by shrewd intimations of health, beauty, or satisfaction? For that matter, how far has the language of commerce, as well as of officialdom in the Pentagon, the State Department, or the White House, become a babel of antilanguage, deceit, falsehood—a verbiage of death, as dehumanizing to those who hear it as to those who utter it? Well, the idolatry of death *is* pervasive in American society, and, I observe, it is connected: each and every manifestation of the power of death, of the moral significance of death in the culture—whether great or little, whether public or private, whether literal or subtle, whether repulsive or tempting, whether notorious or secret—is consequentially related to all other signs and portents of the vitality of death in America.

The first time I saw Anthony Towne was at a party I had been invited to in New York City in honor of W. A. Visser t'Hooft, then General Secretary of the World Council of Churches. Anthony had been engaged as bartender for the occasion—it was a crowded and rather elaborate event—by the host, a mutual friend, Marvin Halverson, the originator of the Foundation for the Arts, Religion and Culture. This happened at a period in my life when I still used alcohol and, indeed, drank enthusiastically; hence, Anthony and I became well acquainted during that evening.

One morning, a few months later, Anthony came to my law office, reporting that he was at that very hour being evicted from his apartment in Greenwich Village. I spent most of the remainder of the day on the matter, but it was by then simply too late to frustrate or forestall the eviction. We did recover Anthony's possessions—books, mostly, and an old typewriter—from the clutches of the sheriff, and in the late afternoon, I suggested to Anthony that he stay at my place pending opportunity to consider the situation. And so our acquaintance became friendship, then, eventually, community.

Sometime before Anthony and I had met, Anthony had suffered a terrifying episode—he referred to it as his "psychotic break"—which, for awhile, had rendered him profoundly apprehensive, morbid, hysterical, dysfunctional. I never probed him about it, but he would mention it now and then, and, occasionally, the experience, or aspects of it, would reprise. These incidents occurred when there was crisis in our household—like when we were being relentlessly, ubiquitously, and, one might add, stupidly harassed, and threatened with imprisonment, because of our hospitality to Daniel Berrigan.

Though I think I did not pry, I gathered, from this and that, that the original episode had much to do with Anthony's response to the death of his father. That had happened while Anthony was young. It was an automobile accident that had killed his father, but Anthony regarded the accident as his father's suicide, and he somehow construed his mother to be morally responsible for his father's death. Anthony's exegesis of his father's death in turn spawned obvious and redundant tensions in the relationship between himself and his mother, although, on his part, those tensions were often repressed, and, usually, she seemed oblivious to the complexity and delicacy of the issues between them.

Parenthetically, I found the situation of Anthony and his parents somewhat bewildering, I suppose because my own relationship with my parents has not been similarly agitated. On the contrary, it has been, for as long as I can recall, straightforward and simple. For one thing, my father and my mother have accorded me autonomy and privacy, even in my days of childhood and adolescence. For another, I love my parents, and I have never had reason to be skeptical about their love for me; but, what is perhaps more relevant, I *like* my parents as people. Therefore (as with other peers of mine who complained of traumatic parental relationships) I encountered and observed Anthony's problems in this realm with a certain dismay and a little surprise, given the benefit of my own parents.

Anthony had been through psychoanalysis and a period of private therapy in the aftermath of his horrors experience, and, by the time that he and I had met, he was still involved in a weekly group therapy session. He was obviously fond of the group and gave high priority to his participation and relationships in it (some of which endured until his death), and he remained in the group until his involvement was preempted by my illness and our decision was made to immigrate to Block Island.

Anthony considered himself alcoholic, and his use of alcohol and its effect upon him was very ambiguous. On one hand, his perception of reality was so sharp and so detailed, so directly felt, so aware, so remarkably intelligent that it was as much a burden as it was a gift; alcohol diminished or subdued that perception, made it seem more ordinary or more bearable, and furnished him some kind of respite from his own brilliance. On the other hand, at times, drinking apparently prompted or induced the reprise of the dread that he had known and suffered. In that experience—insofar as anyone else can speak of it—Anthony was, I think, haunted by an overwhelming apprehension of nonexistence, by the kind of fear of the ultimacy of death that is so momentous that the dread of death paradoxically becomes a dread of living, an immobilizing dread wherein there is no one, there is nothing to identify and affirm who one is or even *that* one is.

The transcendence of the power and presence of death in just such dimensions of dread as these is what the death in Christ, as it has been previously discussed, concerns. The secret of the relationship of Anthony and myself was not that we were able to identify and affirm each other in defiance of dread, but that we were each enabled to apprehend and mediate to the other the truth that the Word of God alone has the ability to identify and affirm either of us as persons or to offer the same to any other human being.

The peril in the experience of dread is in succumbing to the idolatry of death in one's own being. The extent to which this society is death-ridden and the culture motivated by the worship of death, as has been described, constitutes relentless pressure on everyone to surrender and to conform to that idolatry. Those who do conform, die promptly; they die morally as human beings. Anthony did not succumb; he did not conform.

the felicity of Anthony Towne

Shortly after he died, the Block Island Writers Workshop decided to publish an edition of its "Works in Progress" dedicated to Anthony and including some of his poems and prose as "Posthumous Pieces." The Workshop invited me to make an introduction to that part of the journal, which I did, in this way:

> It came to pass that a rare relationship happened to the Block Island Writers Workshop and Anthony Towne, between the time of its beginning and the day of his death.
>
> Members of the Workshop have mentioned him as their mentor—the one among them who was already a

published author and respected poet, whose critique of their efforts was gentle and truthful and seasoned by humility about his own creative writing. And they recall him as their mediator—the one whose discernment and wit would offer a word to the rest apt for the circumstances whether they were of controversy or discouragement or, most fearful of all, success.

What has not been mentioned, and what perchance I alone have known, was the significance of the Workshop to Anthony. It became for him—at the prime of his talent—a way to share who he was and what he knew as a human being with the rest of the world, or at least with some people who valued their own humanity enough to aspire to be civil.

I consider that Anthony regarded the use of the language as the distinguishing feature between that which is civil and human and that which is brutal and dehumanized. The culture, he had noticed long since, had gone the latter way and its debasement of language, indeed, its promotion of jargon, verbosity, redundancy, deceit, doublespeak and similar babel is evidence of a profound decadence. So he was grateful whenever he encountered some civility in people and in society. These are signs of life, he realized, and even of resurrection: indications that the Word of God had not abandoned humanity despite provocations most dreadful.

Anthony Towne struggled poignantly and tenaciously to devote his life and his charismatic gifts to writing. More often than not, the effort was solitary. He was little encouraged in school or family. Poetry is not generally acknowledged as work, though I observed, through Anthony, that it *is* an exacting occupation. At the same time, he considered that there was compromise involved in writing to publish for money. He never sought that, and such of his work that has been published so far was so at the behest of others. He kept no objection to being published posthumously.

Immigrating to Block Island became a turning point in his story as a human being. Creatively, the city had been both stimulant and affront; the ethos and environment of the Island offered nurture and husbandry for his gifts. I do not mean that Anthony romanticized the place, as some do, but that the pace and sounds, the style and sights, the austerity and beauty of the Island consoled him and suited his vocation.

His vocation—as that may be distinguished from his occupation—was, in principle, monastic, as is my own. (That is the explanation of our relationship.) That is, he and I have understood that we had been called to a life of prayer and that the practice of prayer is *essentially* political—a matter of attention to events and of intercession and advocacy for the needs of human life and of the life of the whole of Creation. Prayer, in this sense, is *not* pietistic, but, on the contrary, radical involvement in the world as it is prompted in the Word of God. So coming to the Island to live and work had no connotation of withdrawal or escapism or default for the two of us or either one of us, but, rather, a paradoxical meaning.

Anyway, Anthony came to the Island and his vocation matured and his occupation flourished. He had gratitude for his gifts and he honored them as gifts, despite various obstacles to doing that, and, after awhile, he was free to share his gifts with others as he did, notably, in the Writers Workshop.

I think it premature to tell about my own grief in Anthony's death, except to mention here that I have not found his death, shocking though it be, depressing, or the mourning of his death, maudlin. That is because I know his life to have been fulfilled.

Wednesday next before
Pentecost, 1980

ALPHA

ALPHA
is a is a
nothing not thing
nothing at all no thing not a
from which (ex nihilo) abecedarian generation
may have begotten this universe I am mutely dying (uttering) into
into which by solitary inception was inserted
no death not ever dying never
not dead no dying
is not is
OMEGA

ANTHONY TOWNE

II

Conversion

One poem of Anthony's that did not merely appear posthumously but was widely published during his lifetime and helped establish him as a significant poet was entitled *Dead of Winter*. He died in the dead of winter and, remembering that poem, I believe it was the season in which he would have chosen to die. His cremains (that is an undertaker's jargon) had not yet been returned to the Island by the time the requiem for Anthony was celebrated, so there was no burial that day. Besides, Anthony's mother and his sister and myself had decided to bury his ashes in the lawn near the flagpole at *Eschaton*, and in the dead of winter the ground was frozen; so it seemed apt to wait until spring to return his body to the earth. A burial in the spring would also mean that a day could be chosen when some friends of Anthony who could not attend the requiem could be present. I had discussed this especially with Dan Berrigan and had asked that he preside as priest at the burial.

a "minor exorcism"

In due course the ashes were delivered to me and I placed them in a box on Anthony's bureau to await the event. They had come to me in a vulgar package—a sealed plastic sack that, of course, was not biodegradable. Both theologically and practically, this was an utterly inappropriate way to treat the ashes of a human being, and I began to look for some more suitable and decent receptacle. Father William Wendt, the Episcopal priest whose defense counsel I had been in one of the ecclesiastical trials during the controversy about the ordination of women, learned of this need and presented me with a small pine box, neat and plain and biodegradable, which had been made for Anthony's ashes by some of the artisans of the St. Francis' Burial Society in Washington, D.C. Father Wendt founded this Society, which is engaged in a pastoral ministry to the dying and relatives and friends of the dying. The Society supports this ministry, partly, by making pine coffins. I rejoiced in his gift for I knew Anthony would have been satisfied with it. Meanwhile, a neighbor on the Island offered an antique ship's anchor to mark the grave.

Daniel arrived a few days before the happening, and he and I had time to reminisce. The three of us had been exceptional friends, and, more than that, we had shared in a common pilgrimage. Anthony and I had been thankful that Dan had come to us on the Island while he was being pursued as a fugitive, and we often chuckled, after that whole episode was over and we realized how heavy had been the official surveillance of *Eschaton,* about the conversations the three of us had had that had been overheard (unconstitutionally) by the authorities. Some of them were about the circus as a theological milieu and eschatological metaphor, others were about food and the exchange of recipes, and the significance of the Book of Revelation was constantly a topic amongst us. What would J. Edgar Hoover make of all that? I expect, for all his wild imaginings, for all his solemn fantasies, that he died still in a quandary about such discussions as these into which he intruded surreptitiously.

Dan and Anthony had also had an elite communication arising out of their esteem for each other as poets. I was privy to this, without ever being admitted into it; they both conveyed to me an impression that poets know some basic secret lawyers are categorically unaware of, and which theologians only faintly, occasionally, apprehend. The implication seemed to be that if a theologian somehow achieved insight into the poet's secret, the theologian would thereby become a poet and cease being a theologian. I think I had the permission of Dan and Anthony to overhear their poets' talk because they each hoped I would renounce being a lawyer (I admit it is a profession both decadent and tiresome), and, perchance, then concentrate enough on theology to transcend it and join the poets' circle.

So Berrigan and I recalled Anthony fondly and settled on the form for the burial, relying mainly upon the provisions of the *Book of Common Prayer* because Anthony both loved that book and himself relied upon it. I also asked James Breeden to read some New Testament passages from The Revelation to John. The presence of Jim, an Episcopal priest, and his wife, Jeanne, I particularly anticipated. They had been friends and working colleagues in East Harlem in the late 1950s. Both were students then at Union Theological Seminary and did their seminary field work in the neighborhood. I often made my tenement, on East 100th Street, available to them for their courtship. Pitney Van Dusen once told me that he considered Breeden the ablest student he had encountered while president of the seminary. I had no trouble believing this assessment, because I was supposed to oversee Breeden's field work, and, in these roles, we ended up every Saturday in prolonged and exacting theological discourse. There was for me the bonus that Jim was during that time engaged in reading Karl Barth's *Church Dogmatics* (on his own initiative, not as an assignment). I have never read that (and I do not expect to) but Jim would regularly brief me on his study and advise, sometimes instruct, me as to certain paragraphs that he deemed essential. I would read these dutifully.

For the occasion, furthermore, I chose certain prayers to recite myself. One of these was the commendation for those who "die in the Lord," and others were ancient prayers of exorcism that I had in the Appendices to the study on exorcism that was commissioned in England by the Bishop of Exeter. I do not consider, I should say parenthetically, exorcism to be a superstitious, supernatural, or spooky subject, despite the bizarre fanfare it has lately had in exploitation books, films and talk shows. Biblically the rubric for exorcism is not the occult, but healing, and in the New Testament it is treated in a straightforward and commonplace style, even as it is in venerable liturgies, notably the baptismal rites. To use some of these old prayers of exorcism, in conjunction with the burial of Anthony's ashes, was no more audacious than reciting the Lord's Prayer, and no less appropriate. It meant, simply, an open and public rebuke to the power of death which had lately beset the household and an invocation of the militancy of the Word of God for the ongoing life of the household.

On the day appointed—May 20, 1980—assorted friends and neighbors gathered near the place where earlier in the day there had been dug a space for the pine box. The weather was gray and threatening, but an array of flags had been raised. The ground was consecrated, the Scripture heard, the ashes buried, the dead commended, the power of death rebuked, the household blessed and hallowed, its sojourners yielded to the guardianship of the Holy Spirit.

It thundered—a slow grumble in the sky—and some

rain began to fall. In the esoteric lore of the demonic, that would be noticed as a portent.

retaliation

A few days following the committal of Anthony's ashes to the ground and the observance of the "minor exorcism," I flew into Providence to have one of those laser treatments that had been so confidently recommended to me by assorted physicians as the requisite remedy to arrest diabetic damage to my eyes and to spare my vision. I had submitted to this procedure reluctantly, as I have mentioned, while Anthony had been quite skeptical about the whole idea. The sessions had, despite all qualms, commenced in March, and as they continued, they occasioned in me both staggering fatigue and mounting distress. My attitude, physiologically as well as mentally, toward the treatments was that of resistance—a profound, spontaneous resistance.

The treatments I had found to be so utterly exhausting that I did not attempt, after having one, to return to the Island immediately, but stayed with friends instead, or checked into a hotel to rest until the next day and then attempt the journey. Even at that, when I arrived home I found that I needed further time to recuperate. The distress that was compounding my exhaustion was connected, in part, to the circumstance that I could discern no empirical beneficial result from the laser. Another patient one day remarked to me, "The laser is really a miracle, isn't it?" to which I had to reply, "I don't know, but I don't think so!" There was no basis, in my experience, for any other response. Furthermore, the routine of the treatments seemed to me to be radically dehumanized. That is, I think, a recurrent issue in all medical technology; the laser is a penultimate medical technology. There is no art in it. The physician is reduced to a mere technician: the patient becomes, literally, an appendage of the machine. One is strapped onto the apparatus so that one's body is virtually immobilized and the eye is bombarded, very rapidly, hundreds of times, by brilliant, stunning light flashes, each one of which is a distinct and separate barrage. Perchance the laser *is* therapy—I do not know whether it is or not—but I am certain that it is torture.

The treatment in question took place on a Thursday afternoon. It left me enervated and depressed. I obtained a taxicab at the hospital and went to the Biltmore Plaza Hotel, checked in, went to my room and immediately slept. The next day I flew back to the Island about midday. Still exhausted, I went to bed as soon as I arrived home and slept until early Saturday morning. It was the outset of the weekend in which Memorial Day is now observed and upon which the Block Island School annually holds a fair. Though I felt depleted and vaguely apprehensive, I decided to do a little housekeeping and then, later in the morning, to visit the fair. After breakfast, I vacuumed the rugs in what Anthony and I had called "the common room." At one point I knelt to adjust the machine: I was overcome with a sudden, strange sensation. The left side of my body had numbed. I tried to get to my feet, but I had no balance, and I rolled back on my ass. I waited for some moments, as if to collect my breath, and then managed to rise enough to seat myself in a nearby chair. I stayed there for a long time. The dogs—usually rowdy—came from elsewhere in the house and joined me in the chair. They were gentle. I realized that I had had a stroke.

I had been warned by Dr. Gillie—in the course of his monitoring my diabetes—that I was vulnerable in this way, and that stress, so-called, was to be avoided. I have never received any medical advice about *how* to avoid stress and I sometimes told Gillie that, in my view, once you get out of bed the rest of the day is a matter of stress, so that his admonition was, essentially, gratuitous. Anyway, the only unusual stress that I had experienced lately was the laser procedure. As I sat there that morning—the dogs, with their uncanny intuition, sensing that something was wrong, snuggling me; my left side numb and useless—I also realized that it was most probable that the laser had induced the stroke.

I was stirred from my diagnostic brooding by the sound of a neighbor's automobile coming up the driveway. Frederick Breydert, husband and artistic compeer of (as Frederick spoke of her since her death) "sweet Katharine," entered the house. Having been a victim of the Nazis, Frederick is not readily fazed by suffering or hardship of any sort. I do not mean that he is indifferent to such things, but that he is realistic about them. So he received my brief report of what had just occurred in a matter-of-fact manner. He suggested I see Nurse Donnelly. He did not mention any doctors, because there were no competent doctors on the Island at that time and the nearest mainland hospital, in Westerly, would be on a holiday schedule on the Memorial Day weekend. I asked Frederick to drive me to the School. Mary Donnelly would be, I was sure, at the fair. I shooed the dogs off my lap and rose unsteadily. I was disoriented. My equilibrium was impaired. While standing, it seemed to me that I was about to fall. I tried, with my left hand, to pick up my glasses, but I could not feel them in my hand or control a grip on them and they dropped from that hand. When I left the house with Frederick, my left shoulder involuntarily bumped into the frame of the front doorway. I felt very wary and, as Frederick drove to the school, I worried about what had happened. I recalled the week earlier, when death had been rebuked, openly, in the presence of a congregation, at *Eschaton*. Death, I thought to myself as Frederick parked his car near the school, retaliates promptly.

I wandered through the fair, looking at the various booths and tables and greeting several neighbors and, as it seemed to me, bumping into everything and everyone, so poorly could I navigate my own body. I did not have pain, only the radical loss of sensation and control on my left side. I found Mary Donnelly and described to her what had taken place and how I felt. She found that my pulse was not normal, and from what I had reported, she concurred that I had probably had a stroke. I suggested that I might just rest in bed and wait to see if my left side would improve. Mary insisted that I try to reach Dr. Gillie and find out when I could obtain a thorough examination and, perhaps, hospitalization.

As it happened, despite the holiday, I was able to go over to the mainland to see Dr. Gillie on Monday. By that time there was a slight but discernable improvement in my control of my left arm, but my equilibrium was still awry. The question that most concerned Gillie was whether any permanent or indefinite damage had happened, and he booked me into the Westerly Hospital for a few days for tests. As it happened my hospital roommate there was recuperating from a toe amputation, in consequence of diabetes. He was a retired circus roustabout, having spent many years with the Ringling Brothers and Barnum & Bailey Circus. Since we had both common disabilities and common interests, he and I made good roommates, though I still wonder whether there had been any premeditation in the arrangement. The tests indicated that I could expect a full recovery, but Dr. Gillie advocated that I submit to more sophisticated tests, which the Westerly Hospital was not equipped to do, at a hospital in New London. Though by this time I felt virtually recovered from the stroke, I agreed to do this.

a rehearsal of dying

Afar off I could hear my name. A voice was calling out my name. The voice was not familiar. I could barely hear it; I had to concentrate very hard to make out what the voice was saying. "Bill! Bill!" The strange voice called my name.

I could see myelf quite plainly, my body, that is. My whole body was stretched out, lying, down there. I could see my whole body, but I was up above, as if separated from my body, hovering over the scene, looking down at my body, watching myself.

It was not a dream. It was not at all like a dream. Something else was happening to me.

I was dying.

I realized that I was dying—slipping, slipping, slowly slipping into death.

I felt terribly exhausted. Death seemed attractive, tempting. I could just drift away. Then I could rest.

From wherever I was, somehow detached from myself, I beheld myself. I was lucid; I could perceive what was happening. I could ponder it. I did. I considered my plight for a very long time.

I decided not to die.

I made an enormous effort.

It was an effort so awful, so strenuous, so complete that it could not have been exceeded.

I will not die!

No longer was I anywhere outside myself. I could not watch myself any more.

Then the voice got louder. Very loud. Very sharp like a slap on the cheek.

My eyes opened. I was in bed. People were huddled around the bed. There was a contraption beside the bed, with a bottle, hanging upside down. A tube connected it to my right arm.

"What's that?" I asked.

"Glucose," someone spoke up. I did not like that answer because I knew what it meant.

"We found you on the floor, unconscious, in a coma, a diabetic coma," a voice admitted. It was a voice that I had heard somewhere before. Then I remembered what had happened.

adding insult to injury

Twice, now, since Anthony had died so enigmatically, I had experienced close encounters with the threat of death, and in both instances the specific auspices had been the medical profession and the hospital system.

The stroke, as far as I could conclude, had been occasioned by the distress agitated by the laser bombardment of my eyes and the dehumanized, hi-tech mode in which the procedure had been executed. The eye surgeon (eventually) conceded the plausibility of this conclusion.

The diabetic coma was attributable, quite unambiguously, to the stupidity (to mention nothing more than that) of the hospital regimen. I had been rendered diabetic surgically, thirteen years earlier, as I have related in the book *A Second Birthday*, and during that whole span of time, though I had had familiar problems regulating the insulin in my body, and sometimes had suffered physiological reactions because an excess of insulin had been introduced but had not been utilized, those reactions had never gone beyond tremors or other initial shock symptoms. One must appreciate, of course, if one is not a diabetic, that the kind of prevalent therapy for diabetics is extremely primitive and delicate, influenced by a host of variables about each person and within each person that fluctuate daily and hourly, according to diet, nourishment, exercise, rest, stress, and so on. There is much involved that is little more than guesswork. At best, the current practice of injecting commercial insulin has some immediate stabilizing benefit for the victim to allow him or her to get through a day's efforts with a semblance of normality, but there is little or no long-range benefit in terms of forestalling the gradual, relentless debilitation of diabetes, especially its impairment of the circulatory system.

In any event, I had been conscientious enough for thirteen years in administering insulin daily to myself so as to experience no more than preliminary insulin shocks, which I was able myself to remedy. These have never become so dangerous as to cause collapse, unconsciousness, and coma. I had to become a hospital patient to experience that!

At the hospital in New London I had repeatedly warned doctors, nurses, dietitians, the orderlies who brought meals, and everyone else I could induce to listen, that I was in danger of insulin shock—and all that can follow from it—because my diet at the hospital had been drastically reduced from my routine intake, and the hospital schedule of meals varied so significantly from my accustomed mealtimes. Furthermore, I was not being allowed nourishment as frequently as I needed. At the same time, my insulin dosage, though kept the same in type and quantity, was being administered as much as two hours later than usual. (That meant, if anything, I should eat correspondingly later, but the hospital's convenience called for the final meal of the day to be served at 4:30 P.M. I usually ate dinner three hours after that, and with the late insulin, needed to eat at 9:30 P.M.)

In fact, the night before the coma episode, I had forestalled trouble of the sort because I had brought some food with me. The next morning I had discussed reform of my diet and the insulin dose with those, ostensibly in authority, whose attention I could engage. Complain as I did, attention was nominal, and help was withheld even when the situation became urgent, save a half glass of orange juice someone brought me that was, as the imminent coma proved, too little and too late. Predictably, the response my protests and admonitions elicited throughout that day was "It's not on your chart."

As I regained consciousness, and recalled what had happened, and saw the glucose device pumping sugar into me, I was provoked. Having ignored my warnings before I collapsed, they were now overdosing me as a surety against further insulin reactions. That seemed to me a vulgar precaution.

Well, I did not become a homicide victim in the hospital, and I have heard from other patients—or victims—far more horrific reports than that of what happened to me, but I fear that this sort of thing is endemic in the American hospital system and that most of this is covered up. What outrages me about this literally atrocious situation are not issues of incompetence and negligence of hospital professionals so much as the fact that the hospital system treats the patient as an object, not as a person. It was exactly the same thing that offended me categorically about the laser treatments and how they had been administered. So I reiterate: *dehumanized medicine cannot heal.*

I decided in the middle of the night, as I slowly recovered from the coma, that I had to leave this dangerous place as soon as was practicable. I awaited the results from the various tests and then did depart, wary and angry.

The post-stroke tests showed no evidence of brain damage, but they confirmed that the arteries in both of

my legs were obstructed. This was no news to me—I had
had no feeling in my legs of any kind for about two years;
they were atrophied. Two doctors strenuously argued
that I submit to bypass surgery. They told me it was the
only hope I had of restoring circulation to these limbs. I
listened to what they said. In the circumstances of my
experience in this hospital, they had, of course, a major
credibility problem with me. One of them, leaning over
me, as if confiding a secret, whispered, "If you have this
operation, it will rejuvenate your sex life."

I looked him straight in the face. "All this time I
thought I was celibate," I replied, sarcastically.

a need to pray

When I quit the hospital in New London, I felt acutely
a desire for solitude—for space, for quiet, for privacy. I
wanted to brood; I needed to pray. I sensed that I was
vulnerable. I realized that my life was in crisis, though I
was not in panic. Lately I had twice nearly been done in
by the principalities of commercialized medicine. Yet I
was not in fear of dying; on the contrary, I *knew*, by some
conclusive intuition, that I was *not* going to die. I had, I
suppose, simply resolved not to die, at least not in
consequence of stroke or coma or any similar wiles of the
medical and hospital technocracy. The uncertainties and
ambiguities of my health were not the occasion for crisis;
that had more to do with the event of Anthony's death.
Even so, the crisis was not caused by that death, but had
only been precipitated by it. Hence, for all that had
happened to me since Anthony's death, I was not
demoralized.

When I say I needed space and time in which to brood,
I mean that I had to assimilate what had been taking
place—especially the death, the changes at *Eschaton*, my
health situation—and to assess the various aspects of all

that in an immediate or imminent way, but at the same time I had to relate these recent experiences to my own past and to my own future. I headed back to the Island from New London gladly: I had always found it had a congenial ambiance for brooding.

And when I mention that I needed to pray, I am referring to prayer in what I understand to be its most essential, simple, and rudimentary reality, as a relationship in which the authentic (or, one could say, *original*) identity of a person is affirmed in the Word of God by the Word of God. Prayer, as I mean it, has its integrity in recall of the event of one's own creation in the Word of God.

Prayer, in this significance, is distinguished from the vulgar or profane connotations that have, unhappily, accrued to the term. Prayer, for instance, has nothing, as such, to do with utterance, language, posture, ceremony, or pharisaical style and tradition. Prayer is *not* "talking" with God, to God, or about God. It is *not* asking God for anything whatsoever. It is *not* bargaining with God. It has *no* similarity to conjuring, fantasizing, sentimental indulgence, or superstitious practice. It is *not* motivational therapy, either. It is *not* inspirational. It does *not* seriously resemble yoga, "transcendental meditation," or any other inverted exercises.

More definitively, prayer is *not* personal in the sense of a private transaction occurring in a void, disconnected with everyone and everything else, but it is *so* personal that it reveals (I have chosen this verb conscientiously) every connection with everyone and everything else in the whole of Creation throughout time. A person in the estate of prayer is identified in relation to *Alpha* and *Omega*—in relationship to the inception of everything and to the fulfillment of everything (cf. Romans 1:20, I Corinthians 12:12-13, Revelations 22:12). In prayer, the initiative belongs to the Word of God, acting to identify, or to reiterate the identity of, the one who prays.

Simultaneously, prayer recognizes the identity of God and specifically acknowledges the *godliness* of God. In prayer, construed as a state of being (and not as a religious act), the one who prays is engaged in merely affirming who God is in relation to the acceptance of his or her own humanness.

Now prayer, and the manifold implications of prayer signifying relationships with the totality of the life of the rest of Creation, is the characteristic attitude of the Communion of Saints. I refer, when I use that curious and venerable title, to the entire company of human beings (inclusive of the Church, but transcending time and place and thereby far more ecumenical than the Church has ever been) who have, at any time, prayed and who will, at any time, pray; and whose occupation, for the time being, is intercession for each and every need of the life of this world. As the Communion of Saints anticipates, in its scope and constituency, the full assemblage of created life in the Kingdom of God at the end of time, so prayer emulates the fullness of worship when the Word of God is glorified eternally in the Kingdom.

Prayer, in quintessence, therefore, is a political action—an audacious one, at that—bridging the gap between immediate realities and ultimate hope, between ethics and eschatology, between the world as it is and the Kingdom which is vouchsafed.

In spite of hesitations, relating to the frequent debasement of the term (notaby by professed preachers of the so-called electronic church), I have entitled this chapter "Conversion." That is because prayer is one focus of conversion experience that has the authenticity of biblical precedent. Prayer is elemental to the trauma of conversion, and conversion, at the same time, enables prayer that is, as has been here affirmed, profound political involvement. I beg you, thus, to put aside every stereotyped association with the word *conversion* that you may harbor, and especially so any implications of manipulation, coercion, intimidation, captivation, or delusion that word may secrete. Conversion, biblically speaking, regardless of what huckster preachers may say, concerns the decisive emancipation of a person, in his or her whole being, in the context of the redemptive work of the Word of God throughout Creation. It is that death to self in which the self is liberated.

Part of what I mean when I write that, upon leaving the hospital in New London, I needed to pray, is my recognition at that time that the elements of conversion were implicated in the crisis rendered in my life at Anthony's death. My experience in the aftermath of Anthony's death exemplified and reiterated and ratified my own conversion; this involved specific, historic aggressions of the power of death and the empirical triumph of the Word of God overcoming the power of death. In other words, the truth of my existence, in confronting the fact of Anthony's death, was the drama of death and resurrection. And this was so, not as some abstraction or hypothesis, but as it was mediated and communicated concretely and redundantly in and through events as they happened.

Conversion *always* involves the empirical risk of death; that is why it has little to do with intellectual persuasion or, on the other hand, reaching an emotional high.

Notice some other aspects of conversion: it is always very quaint to speak of conversion because of the mystery of time implicated in conversion. One clue to that mystery is found in Saint Paul when he writes of the categorical and conclusive character of his own conversion and in the next breath talks of suffering conversion every day in a new way (see 2 Corinthians 5:16-17; cf. 2 Corinthians 4:11-12). Another clue is evident in the circumstance that there is no biblical precedent for the notion of momentary or instantaneous conversion. That is a contrivance of so-called mass evangelism. The truth, I suggest, is that time is incongruous in conversion. Time, after all, is a dimension of the bondage to death that all Creation endures, in travail, now, in the era of the Fall. Conversion disrupts that bondage. Conversion interrupts the experience of time. Conversion frees people from confinement in time. Conversion breaks out of the category of time. Conversion enables the transcendence of time. In short, conversion emancipates people from conformity to this world and the regime of time that domineers over the existence of this world.

It is thus paradoxical to refer to conversion in any merely temporal frame, because conversion shatters the calculation of time and relates a person to *all* that has gone before and to *all* that is to come, in the transfiguration, from death to resurrection, of the immediate circumstances. Or, to put it another way, the reality of "time" that prevails in conversion is eternity impinging upon, and actually concluding, the reign of time here and now.

Within the tension between eternity and fallen time in conversion, some experiences of a person may be more prominent or more influential or more edifying than others, but that should not mislead anyone into fantasizing momentary unilateral conversions. Withal, in the midst of the trauma of Anthony's death, and then, especially, in the episodes of stroke and coma, I was strengthened by what had theretofore happened to me in my conversion experience, in my own suffering again of death and resurrection, and (specifically so) in East

Harlem and in my illness in New London, as well as in other circumstances.

on being an heir

The radical self-knowledge that is the gist of conversion is not some attainment of the convert, it is gift wholly attributable to the initiative of the Word of God. This identification of a person in relation to everyone else and everything else in the realm of Creation throughout time—this naming of a person by the Word of God in the Word of God—transcends and transforms every other sort of identification pertinent to that person. It constitutes a person as an heir to the renewal of humanity exemplified in Jesus Christ and as an heir to the whole biblical witness to the consummation of history in the Kingdom of God; or, in another language, as an heir of the Communion of Saints. I have come to acknowledge that status as an heir far more emphatically and to uphold it more conscientiously than I do any other identifications the culture has furnished me with: white, male, American, Episcopalian, Harvard Law, and so on. Anthony had come to a similar sense of being an heir, and both of us had been nurtured in this style of identification, as one might expect, during visits to Israel (to do research for the biography of Bishop Pike). The matter was particularly accentuated on that journey we made together to Israel during the period we were under federal indictment because of our hospitality to Daniel Berrigan, as has been already related in our book *Suspect Tenderness.*

If Anthony felt keenly about being an heir, he simultaneously cared deeply for those who would be heirs after him. Scott Kennedy, who had been our astute aide, guide and counselor on that latter trip to Israel, and his wife, Chris, asked Anthony to be godfather of their firstborn, a son, Peter Jacob. It was an office that Anthony welcomed and that he undertook very seriously (if not solemnly). Promptly upon the child's birth, Anthony began a correspondence with Jacob that continued until Anthony's death interrupted it. This was another way Anthony created of sharing himself that, as I was saying earlier, evinced his readiness to die. This is the first of his letters to Peter Jacob:

Ascension,
1976

Dear Peter Jacob,

Do you mind, by the way, if, in future, assuming there is one, I just call you Jake?

Welcome aboard! I may as well tell you right away that despite the happy circumstances in which you find yourself the plain truth is the human race as a whole is a pretty sorry lot. There are about 4 billion of them and by the year 2000 there may be twice that. I don't expect you to worry yet what they are all going to eat etc. or how they are going to get along with one another. I only want that you should know from the start that it ain't going to be easy. When I came aboard (there were only 2 billion folks around then) things were something of a mess and matters have gone to hell and then some ever since. For all that, though, I must say it has all been fairly interesting. I think you are going to like it.

I had myself geared up to discourse on the facts of life but my theological advisor says he doubts that falls within the purview of my responsibilities. Thank heavens! So, I will say only that the facts of life don't have much to do with the bees, or more precisely the bees (drones excepted) are too busy, apparently, to fuss much about the facts of life, and that may be why most hives, so far as I can tell, are usually harmonious.

Speaking of hives, I take it you are to be raised in a community. I'm sure that is best. We are either going to be communities from here on out or we are not going to be. Still, I am something of an anticommunitarian myself. I may be a sort of closet Thoreau. So, I will say a word about privacy. It is the only luxury I could not do without. It is already as rare as the peregrine falcon. Without privacy poetry becomes impossible, and for that matter pottery. I have been reading about Gandhi in *The New Yorker* (of all places)—excellent three part profile by Ved Mehta in the issues of May 10, 17, and 24—and I am more than ever persuaded that he had the right idea in his cranky, idiosyncratic way. Gandhi, according to Mehta, spent 20 minutes in the morning and 20 minutes in the afternoon on the commode (constipation problems, some think from his vegetarianism), and it was his habit to receive visitors in that posture. Now I rather think Gandhi could have pulled that off, but I doubt many could. You may have to fight for your privacy. Do. Prayer, for example, is private. Beware of folks who tell you their work is their prayer. Prayer is the hardest work there is. Almost nobody does it anymore. Insist on your privacy and use as much of it as you can for prayer.

Now I will comment on the contents of this box.

The maps are to give you some notion of where you are.

The primer is for learning to read. The sooner you start the better. There is too much to be read already in one lifetime and the stuff is being churned out so fast I don't see how one guy can be expected to keep up with it all.

The initials are for establishing an identity. That is important. Especially if you are going to survive in an extended family.

The sunflower seeds mean that when you start something it may seem like there isn't much to work with but really it is astonishing what may come of the matter with persistence (and luck). Besides sunflowers are my favorite flower.

The cross. That is for the baptism, obviously. It was made by the Breyderts, here on the island, Katharine and Frederick. Katharine is 83 years old, and Frederick is 67. Katharine, who is also a retired baby doctor, was insistent that I include some remarks on the cross.

(1) A cross may be worn by a baby if the cross is attached to a ribbon. *Never* a chain.

(2) This cross may be worn by the baby at the baptism but then it should be removed and worn for at least one year by the mother. Thereupon it may be worn by the child "on occasion" and later the child may wear it all the time, if the child person wishes.

(3) This cross is virtually indestructible. It may be smashed

on the floor without suffering damage. It may also be
chewed on without damage but that assurance does not
extend to the teeth involved.

The safety pin. Your mother will know what that's for. The
honey drops are for the picnic.

Give my regards to your (extended) folks.

Love,
"T"

the significance of Block Island

In the months before Anthony's death, I had been
treated to many pressures from those within the
Democratic Town Committee on Block Island to become
a candidate for town office in the 1980 election. After
Anthony's death, these pressures multiplied and diversified. Friends and neighbors throughout the community urged that I run for First Warden, the office of
the presiding member of the Town Council and of the
Warden's Court. This title derives from the seventeenth
century when the wardens of the church were the chief
civil magistrates of the town.

I had served earlier for a term as Second Warden of
the Island. That tenure became controversial, oddly
enough, because I advocated open government. I had
occasion to give an address while in office on "the state of
the Island," which indicates my view of the main
parameters of the controversy:

I believe the message of Island voters in the last election sought
change, sensed impending troubles, apprehended a future that
will not be easy and may not be good. I think that concern
remains—if much unimplemented. I intend to honor it.

What is happening, and what the last election signified,
among other signs, is the ending of an era, in *this* century, in
which the Island has been governed by arrangement in which
some few have made decisions, more often than not in secret,

affecting the many, in which there has been no vital political competition, in which party designations have been subordinate and nominal, and in which paternalism has been a prevailing ethic. . . . There has been an oligarchy, not a democracy, here. For awhile, in this century, it served its purpose. It cannot, however, be said to be the traditional form of government on this Island, for that upheld participation of people in their own government. If I mention, therefore, that there was a conviction expressed electorally last November—an uneasiness concerning the future—it was, ironically, at the same time a call to restore and vitalize the historic and original political ethos of this community favoring participation and representation institutionalized in the Town Meeting and the Town Council.

On the one hand, I meant in those remarks to underscore the truth that the kind of closed, private government that the Island had lately come to have was inherently shortsighted, unable to identify and meet the needs of the Town as a whole; but also, on the other hand, to state my belief that Block Island was one of the relatively few communities left in the nation where it was still a possibility for citizens to participate in their own government. In my conviction, if this be a virtue of the Island—and other similar places—in the contemporary American political scene, to implement that possibility vigorously is also a profound service to the whole of American society. Participatory and representative government responsive to human life and responsible to human beings has been gravely, perhaps fatally, jeopardized, as American society has become programmed by technocracy, conditioned to profligate consumption, dominated by immense principalities indifferent or parasitical toward human life, enthralled and dissipated in overkill war capabilities, glutted and corrupted by overproduction of useless, harmful, synthetic, and ecologically stupid goods and products, exploited and choked by redundant, ugly, indiscriminate, and ersatz overdevelopment, both commercial and residential, coerced and conformed by a reign of lawless authority. Block Island, perchance, is exceptional. Indeed, human discernment needs an exception like Block Island in order to behold the truth about what has happened to America.

Culturally, and especially politically, the nation has descended into a genuine dark age—wrought not by faulted leaders, as plentiful as they are and have been, but in the politicalization of technology since the end of the Second World War—comparable, I believe, to those dark ages which other societies have from time to time suffered. That means, to me, that this is a time to nurture *everything* that can be remembered or conserved or transmitted that signifies civility in humanity. I count literacy, aesthetics, worship, the arts, and politics among such signs, and that is why I have taken Block Island politics so seriously. The Island is still a society—despite what has been happening in so many places on the mainland—where there is an elementary connection between the act of voting and the event of government. That is something worth keeping and nourishing in the midst of a dark age.

I had been elected—to the general astonishment of everyone who noticed—Second Warden of Block Island in 1976, but there had been earlier overtures ventured suggesting that I become a candidate for the Town Council. The earliest of these came in 1970, while my health was very fragile. John Donnelly, a stalwart leader of the Democratic minority in the town, who incidentally shared with me a keen enthusiasm for the circus, approached me about this. I was frank with John about the limits of my energies, but told him that, within those limits, I was not closed to his idea. He was candid with me, too, declaring that he would not anticipate that I could win a Council seat, but that my being a nominee might prepare the way for a later candidacy with more promising prospects of election. As it happened, that was also the summer in which our hospitality to Daniel Berrigan was interrupted by his capture by the federal police. A few days after Dan had been seized, John came by to mention to me that, in spite of his own high esteem for priests in general and Jesuits in particular, he considered that my involvement with Dan had aborted my local political prospects. Neither Anthony nor I disagreed with John's political acumen.

Nevertheless, two years later, John Donnelly returned to renew his suggestion that I stand as a candidate for Town Council. He thought that the Berrigan episode had receded enough by then, and he said he noticed some sympathy and admiration for Anthony and myself in the ordeal of harassment and frivolous indictment that we had been subjected to because of our opposition to the Vietnam War and our friendship for Berrigan. I told John I would think about the matter and we agreed to discuss it further, perhaps being joined in that discussion by other members of the Democratic Town Committee. Meanwhile, I went, before there had been an opportunity for any meeting, to Princeton to address a very large meeting convened at the University in protest of the war. In my remarks there, I argued the case for the impeachment of Richard Nixon as President. It was, of course, more than two years before his resignation, and, indeed, only some months before his overwhelming reelection. Watergate was still covered up. My speech received attention in the newspapers, and when I returned to the Island on the ferry the next day, John Donnelly was there on the dock to greet me. "You blew it again," he said succinctly. "You can't give a speech like that," he handed me a newspaper clipping, "and run for Council here."

In sequel, the following summer, the Watergate hearings chaired by Senator Sam Ervin were telecast. They evoked, as television seldom did, the rapt attention of both Anthony and myself. After the hearings had gone on for some time, one afternoon John Donnelly appeared. He accepted a beer from Anthony and sat down and joined our watch. Several minutes elapsed. John finished his beer. "You know, Bill," he rose from his chair, "that was a good speech you made down at Princeton." Then he left us.

the political temptation

In the hospital in Westerly, after the stroke, I remembered John Donnelly and wondered what his advice to me would be about running, on Block Island, for First Warden in 1980. John (the husband of Nurse Mary Donnelly), had died in 1974. Some of his ideas for strengthening, and reforming, the Democratic Town Committee had by now been effected, and there seemed to be an excellent prospect of electing a working majority of the Town Council on the Democratic ticket; many of my colleagues in the town committee argued that my candidacy for First Warden would help insure a Council majority, whether or not I was myself elected. At the same time, the laser experience and the stroke accentuated qualms I already had, which Anthony shared, about whether my health was sufficiently stable to allow me to run and, perhaps, to serve; or, on the other hand, as Anthony feared, whether running and being elected would debilitate my health.

There were other considerations, too, in deciding whether or not to run. I recognized, for one, that many of the Island folk who were urging me to run were not so much making any political statement, as they were, in this way, saying to me that they hoped I would remain on the Island though Anthony had died. Another aspect to consider was how much the interest in my becoming a candidate was just a sympathetic response to Anthony's death or how much might it be a transference to me of respect and affection for Anthony? That election as First Warden would entail substantial loss of income, just as serving as Second Warden had a few years before, did not weigh as heavily in my thoughts as did the preemption of other concerns—especially writing and speaking—which incumbency would predictably cause.

I am not conscious of there having been any significant issue of personal ambition involved as I deliberated about whether to be a candidate. Such vanity as I suffer from is expressed in other terms than ambition for political office. This might have turned out differently, for I was politically ambitious in my student days. But I had died to that during the time that I was a research fellow in England, at the London School of Economics. It was then that I determined not to pursue politics as a career, and that determination was later ratified when I declined opportunities to run for public office in Massachusetts, where I was raised, and in New York City, while I was working as lawyer in East Harlem. Still my resolve, originated during the London experience, not to fashion a political career for myself was not a rejection of politics or of political involvement. It was really a decision not to expend my life, and such capabilities as I have been given as a person, on *any* career of *any* sort, including politics, specifically because that is the direction in which I was then heading. I realized at that time, in London, that there is no option in this world of abstention from politics: everyone everywhere *is* involved, whether intentionally and intelligently, or by default or some moral equivalent of it. I knew that my decision was not concerned with withdrawal or pietism, but meant that my own political involvements would not be formulated in career terms. I died to political ambition in London, as I have said, and that came about because while I was there, in a quite self-conscious sense, I renounced the notion of having a career—any career—including the goal of having a political career.

Ever since, as one would expect, though I have participated actively in a diversity of ways and roles in the politics of several institutions and communities, as well as that of American society in general, I have regarded politics as a temptation, particularly promptings to run for office. These sentiments were prominent in my mind as the choice about the Block Island candidacy confronted me. In the end, it was my conviction about the Island's significance for America and my conviction about the importance of demonstrating a relationship between the exercise of franchise and the way society is governed that prevailed (albeit amidst a sense of ambivalence and some trepidation that were only dispelled when I learned the election result). The other candidate for First Warden had been elected by a modest plurality in the absentee ballots, but he would preside over a Town Council with a working Democratic majority.

ENDSCAPE

nothing
has been
said about
turning poetry
into prayer although a
point may be made that THE END OF TIME IS TIME ENOUGH for
an alchemy of love
or transmutation of an
empty art form
into words
denoting
nothing

ANTHONY TOWNE

III

Solitude

Anthony Towne was an authentic Renaissance person—catholic in his curiosity, appreciative of tradition and inheritance, both biblical and classical; yet free to contemplate change, alert to creativity, able to distinguish the genuine from the facsimile, the enduring from the transient—and the requiem celebrated at his death was fittingly ecumenical. It featured fragments of his own work. That made the requiem a joy for everyone who gathered for it. Or so it seemed to me.

requiem

The congregation that assembled on January 31, 1980, at St. Andrew's Parish Center, a new facility that had been lately built for the Island's Roman Catholic congregation and for the benefit of the whole community, included most of the people living on the Island during that winter, as well as a goodly number of friends who had come from various places in America, some from great distances, despite the hassles of winter travel between the mainland and Block Island. Margaret Towne, Anthony's mother, who had been present at the Westerly hospital when he died, had, of course, stayed on; as had Joan, Anthony's sister, who had arrived at the hospital not long after his death, accompanied by her husband, George Greiner. George Hey, an old friend of whom Anthony was especially fond, had joined the Towne family.

Scott Kennedy, as I have said, arrived from California, bearing messages from a plethora of friends there, and I was grateful that he was free to remain for a few days with me after the immediate funeral events. Scott had been directly involved in the search in the Judean desert for the body of Bishop Pike, so he was, one might say, uniquely qualified to be a companion in such circumstances. Polly Schoonover, a godchild of mine, had come out of affection for Anthony, and because of her concern for me. Polly, who was then a student at Boston University, also remained for some days following the requiem. She is the daughter of the Rev. Melvin Schoonover, a colleague of mine from the time in East Harlem. I had been best man for Mel when he married Diana Sturgis. Polly, like Mel, suffers from a bone disease and requires a wheelchair to get about, although I notice they are both more effectively mobile than many of the rest of us who do not use wheelchairs. So, with Polly and Scott, and Island neighbors and the pets, I was not without comfort *after* the requiem, in addition to the solace that the requiem itself, and those who participated in it, tendered.

Anthony, Renaissance person as he was, rather liked funerals. He always watched any televised state funerals, typically complaining throughout that this was practically the only appropriate engagement of the medium. (Inaugurations were included in Anthony's television priorities, though I think he regarded them as ersatz funerals.) And he habitually attended Island funerals, even when a deceased was not a close acquaintance, because, he would remind me, these were occasions in which the "tribal lore" of Block Island was recollected, recited, and performed. Such funerals might thus, in some instances, be literally pagan rituals, but still significant culturally whatever their theological status might be. I recall a certain Island funeral service we attended, upon the death of a native Islander whom some deemed a reprobate (though we esteemed him as a person gifted with the insight and courage to tell the truth). The proceedings went on and on for an inconsiderate length, but the minister presiding guilefully managed to avoid even once mentioning the name of the decedent.

Well, Anthony understood the significance of funerals in a comprehensive way and appreciated the decorum of such rites and the heavy irony that sometimes attends them. I was conscious of all this during the discussions with Margaret and Joan and the clergy about how the service for him would be arranged and fulfilled. It would *not* be indulgent or pagan (if I could help it): it would be a mass of the resurrection from death. It would, therefore, be a celebration in gratitude to God for the gift of the life of Anthony Towne. It would remind everyone specifically and personally of Anthony and it would identify Anthony as a beneficiary of Christ's Resurrection. The decision was made to ask members of the Block Island Writers' Workshop to read some pieces Anthony had written, including the obituary that I had found in the Manger and *The Story of Anthony Towne by Anthony Towne,* which had been composed for the Writers' Workshop. The Rev. Anthony Pappas, pastor of the Harbor Church on the Island and a member of the Workshop, prepared an introit for what was to be read by various other Workshop writers.

The remarks of Tony Pappas and the readings from Anthony Towne served as the eulogy. I knew, during the service, that the decision to do this was conscientious when I heard the congregation laugh. This was a good way to express gratitude for Anthony Towne.

The mass itself was ecumenically concelebrated. David Joslin, the priest in charge of the Episcopal mission congregation on the Island, who had spent the hospital vigil with Margaret and Nancy Greenaway and myself, presided. John Seville Higgins, the retired Bishop of Rhode Island, participated, as did the Rev. Howard O'Shea, the Roman Catholic chaplain at Brown University, who had known Anthony from his schooldays at Andover Academy, and the Rev. Robert Randall, the rector of St. Andrew's Church on the Island.

The presence of Bishop Higgins was a particular happiness to me, because he had been bishop and pastor to Anthony and me at the time we were indicted on charges of harboring Dan Berrigan. We had come to have great respect and much affection for the bishop during that experience. We were impressed with his insistence throughout the ordeal that we had done nothing more than practice hospitality as Christians, according to New Testament precedent, just as he would have done in similar circumstances. That episode was refreshed in my mind during the requiem because the bishop was present and also because in the congregation sat Edwin Hastings, the distinguished Rhode Island attorney who had been our defense counsel. Ned had won dismissal of that indictment, because it was constitutionally defective (as political indictments commonly are). Furthermore, Daniel was then thousands of miles away and unable to be present at the requiem. His brother Jerry was there, representing all our Berrigan friends, and serving as one of the honorary pallbearers. The latter were truly honorary, since Anthony had been cremated and there was no body to carry or bury. It was agreed to commit the ashes later, in the spring, after the earth had thawed, at a time when Dan could come to the Island, as I have already mentioned.

Subsequently, the occasional newspaper then being published on the Island by a community education project called SHARE, printed the report of Anthony's death and the requiem, including the selections that had been used as eulogy, along with a touching letter from J. Joseph Garrahy, the Governor of Rhode Island, which an aide of the Governor's had been dispatched to the Island by helicopter to deliver to me at the requiem. In that way, many Island and seasonal folk absent during the winter were able to learn what had happened. Oddly enough, Anthony had written a piece for the immediately preceding issue of the same paper in eulogy of two other persons, much beloved on the Island, who had died: Katharine Breydert and William Gorman.

Most of the requiem congregation gathered afterward at *Eschaton* for a proper wake—I call it that because there had yet been no burial—with food and drink and talk and laughter and sentiment. Then, after a while, I slipped away from everyone. I wanted to be alone. Well, not quite alone: the dogs and the cat assembled themselves and they accompanied me.

sojourn with the circus

The requiem had been a festival, the wake a feast. The gift of the life of Anthony Towne to others had been gladly acknowledged, the resurrection had been celebrated. That night, following the requiem, while the creatures and I were quiet and alone, my memories concerning Anthony were flush and lucid.

One of the bonds between us was that we shared, each in his own style, a sense of absurdity—an instinct for paradox—a conviction that truth is never bland but lurks in contradiction—a persuasion that a Hebraic or biblical mentality is more fully and maturely human than the logic of the Greek mind. The gospel version of the event of Jesus Christ (as distinguished from secular versions of Jesus Christ including those propagated under church or churchy auspices) verifies the significance of this incongruous tension between the Word of God and the common existence of the world (read 2 Corinthians 11, 12). The assurance of faith, in biblical terms, is that we live in that awesome incongruity until it is reconciled *as* the Kingdom of God.

In other words, eschatology impinges incessantly upon ethics. A biblical person is one who lives within the dialectic of eschatology and ethics, realizing that God's Judgment has as much to do with the humor of the Word as it does with wrath.

Anthony understood this, on his own authority, and that is why he abided my attraction to the circus. My most vivid memory, that night after the requiem, was of the year when Anthony and I spent most of the summer weeks traveling with the Clyde Beatty-Cole Bros. Circus through New England and part of New York State.

It was 1966, and there were already signals that trouble with my health was impending. That may have had something to do with our decision to spend the summer the way we did. In any case, we outfitted a station wagon so that it could be used for sleeping, and joined the circus company enroute, booked in a new city each day, traveling late each night in the circus convoy to the next day's stand. As Anthony had foreseen, the experience did not satiate my fascination with the circus as a society, but only whetted it.

It is only since putting aside childish things that it has come to my mind so forcefully—and so gladly—that the circus is among the few coherent images of the eschatological realm to which people still have ready access, and that the circus thereby affords some elementary insights into the idea of society as a consummate event.

This principality, this art, this veritable liturgy, this common enterprise of multifarious creatures called the circus, enacts a hope, in an immediate and historic sense, and simultaneously embodies an ecumenical foresight of radical and wondrous splendor, encompassing, as it does both empirically and symbolically, the scope and diversity of Creation.

I suppose some—ecclesiastics or academics or technocrats or magistrates or potentates—may deem the association of the circus and the Kingdom scandalous or facetious or bizarre, and scoff quickly at the thought that the circus is relevant to the ethics of society. Meanwhile, some of the friends of the circus whom we met that summer may consider it curious that during intervals when Anthony and I have been their guests and, on occasion, confidants, that I have had theological second thoughts about them and about what the corporate existence of the circus tells and anticipates in an ultimate sense. To either I only respond that the connection seems to me to be at once suggested when one recalls that biblical people, like circus folk, live typically as sojourners, interrupting time, with few possessions, and in tents, in this world. The Church would likely be more faithful if the Church were similarly nomadic.

In America, during the earliest part of this century, the circus enjoyed a "golden age." It was the era of P. T. Barnum, Adam Fourpaugh, and the Ringling Brothers, to name but a few of the showmen who assembled extraordinary aggregations of performers, animals and oddities. It was then that the circus was most lucidly an image of the Kingdom in its magnitude, versatility and logistics. There were, for example, few permanent zoological collections in those days, and the circus menagerie was the opportunity for people to see rare birds and reptiles, exotic animals and mammals, wild beasts and other marvelous creatures. Indeed, when the Ringling Brothers advertised their "mammoth million-aire menagerie" as the "greatest gathering since the deluge" it was not a much exaggerated boast. It was similar with the "side shows" or "museums" traditionally associated with the American circus. A separate feature from the main circus performance, the side show originated with Barnum. It assembled and exhibited human "oddities" and "curiosities"—giants, midgets, and the exceptionally obese; Siamese twins, albinos, and bearded ladies; those who had rendered themselves unusual like fire eaters, sword swallowers, or tattoed people. If the side show seems macabre because "freaks" were sometimes exploited, it must also be mentioned that in those days little medical help and few other means of livelihood were available to such persons and that the premise of these exhibits was educational. In any case, so long as they continued they symbolized the circus as an eschatological company in which all sorts and conditions of life are congregated.

It is in the performance that the circus is most obviously a parable of the eschaton. It is there that human beings confront the beasts of the earth and reclaim their lost dominion over other creatures. The symbol is magnified, of course, when one recollects that, biblically, the beasts generally designate the principali-ties: the nations, dominions, thrones, authorities, insti-tutions, and regimes (see Daniel 6).

There, too, in the circus, humans are represented as freed from consignment to death. There one person walks a wire fifty feet above the ground, another stands upside down on a forefinger, another juggles a dozen incongruous objects simultaneously, another hangs in the air by the heels, one upholds twelve in a human pyramid, another is shot from a cannon. The circus performer is the image of the eschatological person— emancipated from frailty and inhibition, exhilarant, militant, transcendent over death—neither confined nor conformed by the fear of death any more.

The eschatological parable is, at the same time, a parody of conventional society in the world as it is. In a multitude of ways in circus life the risk of death is bluntly confronted and the power of death exposed and, as the ringmaster heralds, defied. Clyde Beatty, at the height of his career, actually had *forty* tigers and lions performing in one arena. The Wallendas, not content to walk the high wire one by one, have crossed it in a pyramid of seven people. John O'Brien managed sixty-one horses in the same ring, in what a press agent called "one bewildering act." Mlle. La Belle Roche accomplished a double somersault at great speed and height in an automobile at a time when autos were still novelties.

Moreover, the circus performance happens in the midst of a fierce and constant struggle of the people of the circus, especially the roustabouts, against the hazards of storm, fire, accident, or other disaster, and it emphasizes the theological mystique of the circus as a community in which calamity seems to be always impending. After all, the Apocalypse coincides with the Eschaton.

Meanwhile, the clown makes the parody more poignant and pointed in costume and pantomime; commenting, by presence and performance, on the absurdities inherent in what ordinary people take so seriously—themselves, their profits and losses, their successes and failures, their adjustments and compromises—their comformity to the world.

So the circus, in its open ridicule of death in these and

other ways—unwittingly, I suppose—shows the rest of us that the only enemy in life is death, and that this enemy confronts everyone, whatever the circumstances, all the time. If people of other arts and occupations do not discern that, they are, as Saint Paul said, idiots (cf. Romans 1:20-25; Ephesians 4:17-18). The service the circus does—more so, I regret to say, than the churches do—is to openly, dramatically, and humanly portray that death in the midst of life. The circus is eschatological parable and social parody: it signals a transcendence of the power of death, which exposes this world as it truly is while it pioneers the Kingdom.

a community endeavor

One of the chief topics of talk at the wake, especially among Island neighbors present, concerned the practicalities of my survival living alone on the Island. Some thought that I should not attempt to live by myself, but find a helpmate of some sort. Barely discreet suggestions were ventured. Others insisted that I should each morning telephone the police or rescue squad—or someone—to announce that I had indeed survived another day. A few friends were unaware of the fact that I am a competent cook, accustomed to preparing not merely three, but six meals a day in accordance with my medical regimen. (The reason Anthony, and, for that matter, the dogs have all been overweight—Anthony considered that he had reached "full maturity"—was attributable to their conforming to *my* dietary requirements.)

Meanwhile, I was concerned about the plants. Anthony had been the household's horticulturist, he had a gifted thumb and was very knowedgeable about plants of all sorts. I had difficulty retaining their names, much less information pertinent to their care and nourishment, although I had taken to speaking to the plants in an encouraging manner. I appreciated their presence in the household, and, because they had meant much to Anthony, I wanted them to stay. So I spent some time at the wake interrogating various guests about what was necessary or helpful in nurturing this or that plant.

The chief focus in such conversations about practicalities in my changed circumstances was, however, upon the fact that I did not know how to drive an automobile. I just never got around to learning, and after a time, I tended to regard this noncompliance with the prevailing American macho culture as a virtue. I commented occasionally that it was patriotic not to drive in a society so manifestly and stupidly overdependent upon the overproduction and overuse of the automobile. At the same time, Anthony, who did drive, loathed to do so, especially in America, and deemed the effort supererogatory. We both claimed virtue in our respective relationships to the automobile.

Anyway, it did seem essential to survival, particularly if I lived alone, to be able to drive to the village once a day to fetch the mail and shop and thereby notify everyone else whether or not I was all right. I was willing enough to learn to drive (though I had secretly resolved never to drive on the mainland), and, before the wake was over, I had received eleven offers from various Island friends of driving instruction, plus the tender of the temporary use of two different vehicles. I would have to ponder which offer for driving instruction to accept.

I realized, at the wake, that the issue of driving afforded some Island people a way of conveying their hope that I would not quit the Island because Anthony had died, but make a new way of life for myself on the Island. I appreciated that, especially from those who had volunteered to teach me to drive, but who, nevertheless, might not be qualified for that task.

Verna Littlefield, a very stalwart and patient person, a member of the School Committee, became my instructor. She is, as I sized things up, a matter-of-fact sort of driver herself (I don't think driving is a fantasy experience for Verna; I wanted to eschew *that* dimension of driving).

Through the rest of the winter and into early spring, Verna and I could be seen, usually in the late afternoon, on test drives around the Island. It was, I suppose, some grief therapy for me. And it was a community endeavor, a topic in public circulation, sometimes gratuitously or facetiously, throughout the Island. By the time Fred Benson, one of the Island's most venerable citizens, who administers the driver's examination, decided I was ready to be tested, I had a sense of being cheered on by a throng of neighbors.

Meanwhile, I had disposed of the complex vehicle Anthony had used (it featured four-wheel drive) and had obtained a small car with automatic transmission. I did drive it on the mainland once, when I visited the automobile dealer to purchase it, but that was at the Narragansett Race Track, now abandoned, nearby the dealer's lot, and not on any mainland street or highway.

It had been arranged that the car would be delivered on the ferry by June 1. That turned out, of course, to be just a week after the stroke affecting my left arm. I fretted during that week about whether the consequences of the stroke would render me unable to drive the car. The delivery day arrived, the car had voyaged safely, under the watchful custody of some mainland friends who had volunteered to accompany it. The ferry crew removed it from the vessel, parking it near where I stood on the dock, and handed the keys to me. I got in, sitting in the driver's seat. My mainland friends climbed in, too. There were a number of Island folk gathered on the dock. They were watching to see what would happen next. I drove away, and, as I did so, I could hear some cheers among the people on the dock.

an island is a ghetto, too

The consideration of my Island neighbors for my practical well-being in the time immediately after Anthony's death, conveyed to me in part through the episode of learning to drive, caused me to realize how similar, as a community, Block Island is to East Harlem. Superficially, of course, these seem to be very different places—the one still rural, underdeveloped, sparse, and, of course, at sea; the other a penultimate urban scene, ruined, congested, a slum. Yet the similarities, of a substantial character, are striking. Both are essentially villages, with highly self-conscious inhabitants. Both nurture strong identities standing over against the rest of the world, Block Island as distinguished from the mainland or America, East Harlem as distinct from the rest of the city outside the ghetto. In both there is astonishing internal communication—grapevines—that informs more or less everyone about more or less everything more or less instantaneously. Once accepted—though that may be a complex and subtle initiation—a person is safeguarded in many ways simply by being a member of the community. In both an ethic of privacy survives, along with a neighbor ethic sensitive to common needs. In short, according to my experience, both Block Island and East Harlem are communities that function as extended families.

Block Island and East Harlem share many problems, too, not the least being those associated with the economic dependence of each on the rest of American society and the extent to which both are exploited regions within American society. One cannot be optimistic about the future of either place, though I believe one may nonetheless live in hope. Hope means something quite different from optimism—in fact, hope is virtually the opposite of optimism. This is to say, simply, that optimism refers to the capabilities of principalities and human beings, while hope bespeaks the effort of the Word of God in common history. Moreover, that distinction signifies that hope includes realism, while realism undermines or refutes optimism.

One day, while I was loitering at the airport, I overheard a conversation of some people—mainlanders—as they awaited an airplane that was to fly them, as I gathered from what they were saying, into New York City. When the pilot summoned them to board the plane, one of them turned to his companions: "Oh, well," he exclaimed, "back to reality!"

I stifled my impluse to protest his remark, and allowed them all to depart the Island in ignorance. But, at the same time, I thought to myself: *Anyone who has ever received a bill from the Block Island Power Company knows where reality is.*

That visitor's sentiment concerning Block Island bespeaks a very common view among tourists and seasonal residents, and, I observe, it is as much an attitude of many Islanders and year-round folk.

The *real* world is over there—on the mainland—in America. *Reality* is in New York City and in Washington, D. C., and in Providence and Warwick, and (as it most assuredly *is*) in Westerly.

Block Island is somewhere else—in a different dimension of space or time or both. Block Island is like a residue from another century. I know someone here who tells me he came to the Island originally, two dozen years ago, because he wanted to live in the eighteenth century and this was the nearest he could come to it. Anthony Towne suffered a somewhat similar exceptional nostalgia; at the least, he withheld his assent to the twentieth century.

The Block Island Chamber of Commerce, I notice, in its literature indulges this same attitude, which it considers, I suppose, an exploitable economic asset, though it refers to the nineteenth century—"a Victorian idyll"—as the ethos in which Block Island is found.

The *Providence Journal-Bulletin* nourishes impressions of this sort by its periodic reports, not about life here, but an image of life here construed as amusing or interesting, eccentric or quaint, when compared to the seriousness, importance, sophistication, and solemnity of mainland culture and society. And if one has noticed how condescending the *Journal-Bulletin* generally is in its stories of Block Island, I trust one will also realize that condescension is a form of exploitation.

Block Island is an escape from the tumult and complexity and congestion and anger and noise and overdevelopment and decay and pollution and motion and waste and babel and competition and fatigue and violence and harassment and conformity and danger of the mass, urbanized and suburbanized, American technocratic regime. Persist in this way of thinking of Block Island and Block Island becomes Fantasy Island.

Yet I say that reality is on Block Island, now, in the twentieth century, not in some facsimile of another era. Block Island is not a mythological realm. As a theologian, I treasure myth and know something about the significance of myth. Myth is helpful when it enables discernment of the truth, but myth is harmful and, even, dehumanizing, when it inhibits coping with reality.

The reality of Block Island now is sobering, just as it is

for the rest of America and for the rest of the world. That is, in part, because the essential issues here and elsewhere are profoundly similar. If matters vary here in scope compared to the mainland, the difference is compensated for in the intensity with which questions are focused on the Island.

The singularity of issues, as between the mainland and the Island, is most apparent in the imminence of nuclear calamity of apocalytic scale in which all humanity, and indeed, the whole of Creation now lives. That calamity is the penultimate shadow impending over everyone and everything. It portends a grotesque consummation of all war, plague, catastrophe, holocaust, and chaos that has ever happened. There are those in high office who talk pompously of "limited nuclear strikes" and "acceptable risks" of tens of millions of casualties, but I suggest that anyone capable of such bizarre calculations is patently insane—in the old legal meaning of insanity as loss of conscience, or moral disability.

All of us may die as nuclear fatalities before madness has time to implement such wicked games, because the nuclear arms race—in which more than twenty nations are now entered—has a momentum of its own outside the control of technocrats, scientists, military professionals, or, perchance, the direction of governments—much less the influence of ordinary citizens. In any case, Block Island is no escape from nuclear reality; in fact, it is directly within high-priority targeted regions and is utterly vulnerable.

If Block Island is not decimated, its next most probable destiny is its depopulation and disappearance as a full-time community. And if the Island ceases to be a viable society year round and becomes merely a seasonal resort, then that manifestation of Block Island will predictably become, more and more, a facade or a replica—a put-on for the visitors—of the same genre, in principle, as Disneyland, Mystic Seaport, or, should the Island become classy enough, Williamsburg. But Block Island will disappear.

The seasonal commercial trade needs the civilizing basis of an authentic, historic, living community and of a viable year-round economy in order to have integrity; in order to be, humanly speaking, worthwhile; and in order to spare the ethos of the Island from raw exploitation. The threat of the expiration of the winter colony has been evident for some time and has been accentuated lately (since about the time that Block Island was rediscovered by the *New York Times*). Hardy as *we* are, the numbers who live here all year dwindle annually, and the human costs of winter survival become harsher each year.

Some causes of this situation can be identified, though they are not neat and, in reality, they are long-term, mixed up, complex, and interconnected with the demoralization of society on the mainland.

One factor is that Block Island has a desperate balance of payments problem. A huge volume of cash—profits, income and taxes—is generated each summer on the Island, but most of it leaves the Island and prospers the mainland. A relatively modest amount remains to circulate here in the wintertime, to provide goods and services and jobs so much needed when the resort season ends. Every dollar that does remain here to circulate is actually worth six times as much because it is exchanged that often. In short, the economic relationship between mainland and the Island is parasitical, and the Island is the victim.

A corollary to this is the Island's overdependence upon imports. At the turn of the century, the Island produced its own food and fuel and energy (or else it did without).

If it was not self-sufficient, it was at least self-reliant. And it was able to support not only a thriving resort commerce, but a full-time community with thrice the population that there is now, employed in a diversified economy. Overdependence upon imports, both basic and superfluous, has been convenient, as long as imports were cheap and transport was inexpensive, but those days have passed, long since. If the Island cannot not identify indigenous resources of food and fuel and energy, create jobs utilizing the Island's own resources, and begin to export Island products, the Island faces extinction as a year-round economy and community.

In the summer of 1980, an edition of the *Block Island Times,* with its accustomed hyperbole, announced that the Island was in the midst of a great economic boom. The truth is the "boom" is only a balloon—fragile, inflated, and vulnerable to a pinprick or a spark. The single most valuable asset of the Block Island economy is underdevelopment: the natural environment, the open spaces, the beachways, the wetlands, the bluffs, the Island's wild ecology. Such things have become so scarce in America, especially in the Northeast, that access to them becomes expensive here. So land values escalate, the land is bought and sold and developed, and each time that happens, though quick profits are taken, the Island's rudimentary asset is depleted and diminished. Moreover, the expense of living on the Island increases for everyone as the demand for energy capacity and municipal services rises. That burden falls disproportionately on those who pay this overhead year-round. At the same time, the full-time community does not grow because the escalation in land values makes homesteading prohibitive. Block Island is caught in a cyclical kind of development that squanders the future of the Island.

Yet I do not consider this a melancholy message. It is a plea for realism. As I was saying, hope is conceived in the truth, not in myth, fantasy, or fairy tale.

an edifying catechism

I recognize that one way to construe my affirmations of the communities of East Harlem and Block Island, and of their similar virtues, is as *church*. The life of these communities—as I have known them—resembles the society that the Church is called to be in the world. At the least, this is true of East Harlem and true of Block Island at some times. The same rubric explains my seriousness about the circus; the circus often seems to me to bear more characteristics of the Church than the professed church can claim. Indeed, much the same can be affirmed concerning *any* society. Every society aspires, no matter how tawdry or ambiguous it is, to be the Church. This is just another version, put backwards, of the confession that the Church is called to be the exemplary principality in the midst of fallen Creation.

A few years ago, some parents asked me to give confirmation instruction to their children, in the absence of an Episcopal priest on the Island. I agreed, with the bishop's authorization, to do so. I almost immediately lamented that decision when I examined the materials currently being published by the established churches, like the Episcopal Church, for these purposes. The stuff was theologically untrustworthy. The day of the first class I informed the children that we would not be using any curriculum, but in its place we would do some Bible study in the Book of the Acts of the Apostles, because it reports the precedent of the Church historically, and because the purpose in the class was to find out what it meant to be a consenting and witnessing member of the Church. We would also review the catechism, as it is set forth in the

Book of Common Prayer, to see if we could make any sense
of it. (Oddly, I had once had a somewhat similar occasion
to become involved in Bible study with some East Harlem
adolescents; that experience is related in detail in *Count It
All Joy.*) Toward the conclusion of the class, which had
ten sessions during which we managed to read the first
four chapters of Acts, I asked each of the students—they
were all either eleven or twelve years of age—whether or
not there was any reason for the Church to be on Block
Island, in view of what the class had discovered the
Church to be from reading in Acts. They were
unanimous, some rather strenuous, in the opinion that,
because the community as a whole acted so much like the
Church, there was no special cause to have a separate
institution on the Island that professed the name *church*
(and certainly not four churches). Now Providence, and
other places on the mainland, of which they had
knowedge almost exclusively via television, was different, they volunteered: Providence really needs the
presence of the Church.

Later I shared their insights with Anthony. He readily
agreed with them, both about Block Island and
Providence. I did, too.

St. Ann's-in-the-Sea

Nevertheless, in due course, they were each confirmed
in the Episcopal Church. Some have remained on the
Island and become involved in the curious little
congregation, or paracongregation, that professes to be
the Episcopal Church on Block Island. When it was
organized, it took the name St. Ann's-by-the-Sea and in
due course a small church building, featuring a
sanctuary, was constructed. The congregation is said to
have flourished modestly for many years until the Great
Hurricane of 1938, which was devastating for Block

Island. In that storm, St. Ann's Church literally blew away. Ever since, Island wags have referred to it as St. Ann's-*in*-the-Sea. The congregation remained moribund in the aftermath of this hurricane, which, after all, was officially designated "an act of God."

Then, about a dozen years ago, St. Ann's began to revive. Initially, people—including recent immigrants to the Island like Anthony and myself—gathered as a house church, reciting the daily offices, or, occasionally, antecommunion, doing some Bible study, and discussing the news of the Island and of the world. Once in a while a priest would visit and there would be Holy Communion. Free of the usual parish encumbrances of organization and property, the house church gradually attracted more and more people, and in the summer weeks, it seemed appropriate to begin to have weekly services with a visiting priest at the site of the ruins of the building that had been demolished by act of God in 1938.

That may have been a fatal decision. Since then, the congregation has been canonically recognized as a mission of the Diocese of Rhode Island, the traditional polity for missions has been instituted, and, predictably, the sentiment for rebuilding has steadily increased. We do not do Bible study any more; we do not seriously consider the mission of the Church in the world, including Block Island; we seldom ask any ecumenical questions. We are into raising money, which we will likely spend to embellish the social life of Episcopalians and their kindred in the summer colony. Has anyone ever heard this story about the Church before?

Anthony and I and some few others became dissenters from the prevailing attitude in St. Ann's-in-the-Sea, with its ecumenical indifference and preoccupation with property and pretense. We have understood all this to signal the process of radical secularization that the

Episcopal Church—in common with the other "established" churches in America—suffers. There has been a basic surrender to the culture in which the preservation of the ecclesiastical institution and fabric *for its own sake* has acquired a priority that trivializes the gospel of Jesus Christ and scandalizes the Apostolic precedent of the Church.

has God abandoned the Church?

The metamorphosis through which the Church is secularized is the same as that by which the gospel is rendered religious. When all is said and done, both aspects of this remarkable change are rooted in denial of the viability of the Word of God in this world. The pioneer Christians were not insulated either from the temptation to conform, as the Church, to the prevailing culture and regime in society, or from emulating the practice of religion, as the New Testament amply verifies (see, e.g., Galatians). Still, by the time of the Constantinian Arrangement, the secularization of the Church and the religionizing of the gospel became dominant in Christendom in the West. Søren Kierkegaard was, much later, to use the name *Christendom* to distinguish the worldly conformity of the Church and the religious corruption of the gospel from the freedom characteristic of the company of confessing Christians living in the world in reliance upon the militance of the Word of God. And, only recently, we have heard the testimony concerning the biblical integrity of religionless Christianity from Dietrich Bonhoeffer. My old friend Jacques Ellul is a companion in this witness. Among a host of others, so was Anthony Towne.

I was, therefore, really not surprised to find, among Anthony's papers, after his death, a correspondence he had had during the last couple of years with Frederick

Beldon, who was Bishop of Rhode Island during the period these letters were being exchanged. Bishop Beldon died only shortly before Anthony did, in the midst of the correspondence, but one imagines that they have continued their dialogue elsewhere. The focus of the letters is upon the current separation of faith and church. Anthony questions whether, if one has faith, one can conscientiously belong to a church like the Episcopal Church, with its pretentious regalia of decadence. He suggests that people of biblical faith are consigned, in this day, in this culture, to extemporizing the Church from day to day in the circumstances in which they find themselves—in various households, in prison cells, on the streets, among the sick, the poor, or the outcast, and, for that matter, on islands. Bishop Beldon is, in his contributions to the dialogue, not defensive about the Episcopal Church; in fact, he is disarming, for he sees the renewal of the Church happening with great vigor and diversity in the world and hopes that, with all its admitted worldliness, the Episcopal Church will also know renewal now and then, here and there.

The issue underscoring the Towne-Beldon letters, if put more sharply than either poet or bishop did, is the question of abandonment: is the present apostasy of the Episcopal Church (and the other, similar churches of the establishment) such that it can be discerned that God has abandoned the Church?

If the question sounds strange in our ears, it is because American Christendom is so complacent concerning the behavior of the Word of God. We suppose that God is indefinitely patient. And we construe this as a license for infidelity to the Word of God. Then we succumb to the temptation to so identify the Church with God that we act as if the Church *is* God. *That* idolatry of the Church is the most incongruous and absurd form of apostasy.

I have no doubt that God is duly patient, but there is no scriptural basis for the notion that God's patience is inexhaustible. On the contrary, as soon as the office of God in Judgment is affirmed, it has been acknowledged that the patience of God is not indefinite. And so, in the biblical witness, there is emphatic mention of the anger of God, the wrath of God, the vindication of God, the vengeance of God (Matthew 25:31-46). More than that, the very event of Jesus Christ in history discloses the impatience of God with the infidelity of the professed people of God. God does not foreswear God's own initiative in common history merely because of the apostasy of the ecclesiastical principalities that profess relationship with God. Following the account of Pentecost, the New Testament is redundant in its warnings to the new congregations concerning the impatience of the Word of God as they become tempted by vainglory, religion, idolatry, conformity, and similar dissipations (e.g. Corinthian letters). Today we remain privy to those same admonitions.

a song of hope

The issue of abandonment is no esoteric theological matter. It is preeminently an existential question that commonly plagues persons at the time of death and was uttered by Jesus himself from the Cross.

When I was an adolescent, precocious as I then may have been, the mystery of the Incarnation much exercised my mind. At the time in life when (I suppose) I should have been obsessed with football, sex, or pop music, as my peers seemed to be, I was very bothered about the identity of Jesus—preoccupied by issues of who he was and who he is—particularly by the matter of the relationship *in* Jesus Christ of humanity and deity.

I do not know—yet—how to account for this preemp-

tive, and passionate, curiosity that disrupted my youth. I
had not been treated in my upbringing, in either family
or church, to sectarian stereotypes of Jesus as chum or
sentimental intimate. Indeed, I regarded these as vulgar,
possibly perverse, and certainly pretentious familiarities,
denigrating to Jesus, even though they often induced for
the indulgent ecstasies equivalent to a high attained
through alcohol or drugs. I had suffered, instead,
prosaic indoctrinations that asserted the "humanity of
Jesus," while simultaneously alleging the "divinity of
Christ." Such instructions had left me with a strong
impression that Jesus was an extraordinary schizo-
phrenic. Meanwhile, adoptionist notions that I heard
rumored I rejected as probable sophistry since they
seemed impotent to dispell the essential incoherence of
dogma. In the congregation I received comfort from the
introit of The Gospel According to John, which was
recited at the end of every eucharist, because it seemed to
affirm the integrity—and indivisibility—of the life of the
Word of God in this world, and to do so in appropriate
syntax (see John 1:1-14).

Perennially this concern of mine would find focus in
the reports in the Gospels of the Crucifixion of Jesus,
especially the reference to his cry: "My God, my God,
why hast thou forsaken me?" (Mark 15:34; cf. Matthew
27:46). Oh, dreadful words! Ghastly question! Pathetic
lament! Ultimate despair! Exquisite agony! This is *Jesus*
crying out. *Why* would Jesus speak this way? *How* could
Jesus do so?

Then, one Good Friday while I was still in high school,
I heard a preacher, more edifying for the laity than
others had been, remark that these words of Jesus from
the Cross were the opening verse of Psalm 22.

My God, my God, why hast thou forsaken me

and art so far from saving me, from heeding my groans?
O my God, I cry in the day-time but thou dost not answer,
    in the night I cry but get no respite.

Psalm 22:1-2

Later that same day I read the Twenty–second
Psalm—perhaps a hundred times—but it did not quiet
my agitation. I still had all my questions, although I recall
that the effort distilled them: Why had not Jesus begun
the recital of the Twenty-*third* Psalm, rather than the
Twenty-second (like, I thought to myself, more or less
everybody else does at the moment of death)?

And yet thou art enthroned in holiness,
    thou art he whose praises Israel sings.
In thee our fathers put their trust;
    they trusted, and thou didst rescue them.
Unto thee they cried and were delivered;
    in thee they trusted and were not put to shame.

Psalm 22:3-5

It was some time after I had exhausted my adolescence
when I began to hear the Twenty-second Psalm as a
hymn of eschatological hope, rather than a dirge of
ultimate despair. If it is concluded that the outcry of
Jesus from the Cross attributes the whole of Psalm 22 to
Jesus, then one evidence that hope is the topic, rather
than despair, is the radical identification of Jesus with
Israel. And this is not simply a matter of inheritance, of
Jesus indicating that he shares in Israel's heritage and
custom—as had frequently happened in earlier episodes
in his life, going back to the time of his circumcision. But
in the midst of the Crucifixion, much more is involved;
the identification relates to Israel's vocation as the holy
nation called in history to recognize the reign of the
Word of God in the world and to pioneer the praise and

worship of God as Lord of Creation on behalf of all
nations, tribes, peoples, and principalities. And, even
more than that, the connection between Jesus and Israel
signified in the psalm concerns the disposition of Israel's
vocation. Thus, condemned by the Roman rulers,
defamed by the ecclesiastical authorities, disfavored by
the multitudes, betrayed, denied, abandoned by disciples, friends, and family; reviled, rejected, humiliated,
utterly beset, crucified: Jesus, crying aloud from the
cross, speaks *as* Israel. In that moment, there is nothing,
there is no one left who is Israel except Jesus. He is, then,
"King of the Jews," as the indictment affixed to the cross
states; but he is, at the same time, within himself, the
embodiment of the whole people of God, and he alone,
then and there, assumes and exemplifies the generic
vocation of Israel to trust and celebrate the redemptive
work of the Word of God in history. In the drama of the
Crucifixion, Jesus' invoking the Twenty-second Psalm
signifies that the Cross is the historic event in which Jesus
Christ *becomes* Israel.

> But I am a worm, not a man,
>   abused by all men, scorned by the people.
> All who see me jeer at me,
>   make mouths at me and wag their heads:
> "He threw himself on the Lord for rescue;
> let the Lord deliver him, for he holds him dear!"

Psalm 22:6-8

Another way to behold the peculiar and intense
identification of Jesus with Israel's vocation is in terms of
the historic fulfillment of that which is written. Jesus was
conscientious about this throughout his public ministry,
from the time of his first appearance in the synagogue—
and his reading from Scripture there (Luke 4:16-30; cf.

Matthew 13:54-58, Mark 6:1-6). What is involved in this, so far as I understand, is not some simplistic or mechanistic process, but faithfulness in the performance of the witness to which one is called. So, here, the words from the cross foreshadow the scenario of the psalm, while the psalm portends the event of the Crucifixion, so that the narrative of the Crucifixion in the Gospel accounts becomes a virtual recital of the psalm.

But thou art he who drew me from the womb,
    who laid me at my mother's breast.
Upon thee was I cast at birth;
from my mother's womb thou hast been my God.
    Be not far from me,
for trouble is near, and I have no helper.
A herd of bulls surrounds me,
    great bulls of Bashan beset me.
Ravening and roaring lions
open their mouths wide against me.
    My strength drains away like water
    and all my bones are loose.
My heart has turned to wax and melts within me.
My mouth is dry as a potsherd,
and my tongue sticks to my jaw;
    I am laid low in the dust of death,
    The huntsmen are all about me;
    a band of ruffians rings me round,
and they have hacked off my hands and feet.
    I tell my tale of misery,
while they look on and gloat.
They share out my garments among them
and cast lots for my clothes.
But do not remain so far away, O Lord;
O my help, hasten to my aid.
Deliver my very self from the sword,
    my precious life from the axe.
    Save me from the lion's mouth,
    my poor body from the horns of the wild ox.

Psalm 22:9-21

The psalm bespeaks one utterly assailed by the power of death: beset by the pervasiveness, militance and versatility of death; bereft of any ability to cope with death. The psalm bemoans the agony of death by crucifixion: the psalm bespeaks the helplessness of humanity against the relentlessness of the great array of death. *I am laid low in the dust of death.*

That is the human destiny; more than that, that is the destiny of the whole of Creation, apart from the event of the Word of God in history. And it is that radical confession of helplessness that is at once the preface of faith and the invocation of the grace of the Word of God. Sin is, actually, the idolatry of death. The last temptation (in truth, the *only* one) is to suppose that we can help ourselves by worshiping death, after the manner of the principalities and powers. That final arrogance must be confessed. Jesus confessed that in our behalf when he cried aloud from the cross. When that confession is made, we are freed to die and to know the resurrection from death.

The recital in the Apostles' Creed, *He descended into Hell,* has a similar significance: Hell is the realm of death; Hell is when and where the power of death is complete, unconditional, maximum, undisguised, most awesome and awful, unbridled, most terrible, *perfected.* That Jesus Christ descends into Hell means that as we die (in any sense of the term *die*) our expectation in death is encounter with the Word of God, which is, so to speak, already there in the midst of death.

> I will declare thy fame to my brethren;
>> I will praise thee in the midst of the assembly.
>> Praise him, you who fear the Lord;
>> all you sons of Jacob, do him honor;
> stand in awe of him, all sons of Israel.
>> For he has not scorned the downtrodden,

nor shrunk in loathing from his plight,
nor hidden his face from him,
but gave heed to him when he cried out.
Thou dost inspire my praise in the full assembly;
   and I will pay my vows before all who fear thee.
   Let the humble eat and be satisfied.
   Let those who seek the Lord praise him
   and be in good heart forever.
Let all the ends of the earth remember
   and turn again to the Lord;
let all the families of the nations
   bow down before him.
   For kingly power belongs to the Lord,
   and dominion over the nations is his.

Psalm 22:22-28

The outcry from the cross is no pathetic lament, but a song for Easter. And the hope it expresses is not vague, illusory, or fantasized, but concrete, definitive, and empirical. The Twenty-second Psalm (hence, Jesus on the cross) manifests that hope in political terms. The influence of the psalm on the Crucifixion accounts underscores the political character of the Crucifixion. The psalm elaborates the politics of the Cross.

Any public execution is, obviously, a political event in a straightforward and literal sense, but the public execution of Jesus Christ has political connotations of immense, complex, and, indeed, cosmic scope. This becomes apparent, for example, when the images of the psalm portray the powerless victim threatened by predatory beasts, a familiar biblical way of denominating political principalities and powers. It is, after all, in the name of Caesar, the overruling principality, that the sovereignty of the Word of God over Creation is disputed and mocked (cf. Luke 23:1-2; Matthew 22:15-22; Mark 12:13-17; Luke 20:19-26; Matthew 27:27-31; Mark 15:16-20; John 19:1-3).

The political reality of the Crucifixion is accentuated in the psalm where it is announced that the cry of the forlorn is heard and heeded (Psalm 22:24*b*). Notice the circumstances: the scene is the Judgment, with the whole of Creation in assemblage, and with all who fear the Lord of history praising Him. Let it be mentioned here that the attribute that chiefly distinguishes Christians is, simply, that they fear the Lord *now*, or already—before the Day of Judgment. That means specifically that they acknowledge that they live and act in the constant reality of being judged by God. Thus, nowadays, when people assemble as congregations in praise and worship of the Lord, this is an anticipation or preview of the Judgment. Where, instead, the regime is glorified, superstition prevails, or religiosity is practiced, then the congregation indulges in scandalous parody of the Judgment.

Notice as well that in the context of the psalm, the event of the Judgment is, so to say, the *first* day that the downtrodden are no longer scorned (Psalm 22:24*a*). For the poor, the diseased, the oppressed, the dispossessed, the captive, the outcast of this world, the Day of Judgment in the Word of God means not only the day of justice, but also the day of justification, when their suffering is exposed as grace.

The politics of the Cross delivers a message to the nations, to all regimes and powers, and even unto the ends of the earth, marked by the cry of Jesus that invokes the psalm: *kingly power belongs to the Lord, and dominion over the nations is his* (Psalm 22:28). *That* is truly what the Incarnation is all about.

> How can those buried in the earth
>   do him homage,
> how can those who go down to the grave
>   bow before him?

> But I shall live for his sake,
>   my posterity shall serve him.
> This shall be told of the Lord to future generations;
>   and they shall justify him,
>   declaring to a people yet unborn
>   that this was his doing.

Psalm 22:29-31

In the psalm, the last word in the cry of Jesus from the cross is an assurance of the efficacy of the Resurrection. To become and be a beneficiary of the Resurrection of Jesus Christ means to live here and now in a way that upholds and honors the sovereignty of the Word of God in this life in this world, and that trusts the Judgment of the Word of God in history. That means freedom *now* from all conformities to death, freedom *now* from fear of the power of death, freedom *now* from the bondage of idolatry to death, freedom *now* to live in hope while awaiting the Judgment.

END TIME

Marigolds like candelabra quiver nonchalant as dead rain
Falls upward from fields the sheep have crunched
And I, incurious and middle-aged, recall
How making love was once the way
Time ending opened fully
In the irregular
Eschaton
Regularity later
Topsy-turvied exactly as
Her dime store paperweight, when
Shaken up, became snow sheep quivered in
And in a crunching of time the pewter candelabra
Became no grandmother, a nonchalance of marigolds dying.

ANTHONY TOWNE

IV

Joy

Nearly a year had elapsed since Anthony's death, but there lingered aspects of my grief with which, I knew within myself, I still had to cope. I do not expect my grieving at the loss of Anthony to be fully spent until the very Day of Judgment, as I have already said, but I realized as the anniversary of his death approached that I had to be released from grief—to break out of its parameters—in order to honor my vocation. Whatever happened I would not, I dared not, become a hostage to grief.

Anthony had been my sweet companion for seventeen years, but grieving for myself because he had died was neither tribute nor benefit to him and should not become the purpose or the focus of my existence.

let the dead bury the dead

There was more implicated here than a matter of the temptation of a bereaved person to live in the past, and more than the vanity of indulgence in self-pity. There was, as well, the issue of allowing grief, the atmosphere and activities of grieving, and the effort of grief, to define my living. If I allowed this, the power of death would not only have claimed Anthony in the grave but would also seize me—prematurely, or without sufficient pretext. To exist only to grieve, to live only to bemoan my loss, would mean my dying morally as a human being. That would be an ignominious way to die. I knew, by now, the only way to affirm Anthony in death, that is, the only way to mourn Anthony, as distinguished from grieving, the only way to continue to articulate my love for Anthony, would be in being freed from grief.

A signal of my need in all of this, it seemed to me, was the fact that I had, in the time since Anthony had died, not yet wept. I had shed tears at the hospital while Anthony was dying, but I had not wept in grief. I had not even wept at the requiem. On the contrary, the requiem had prompted my laughter and had filled me with elation. And since then, with time off for the laser treatments and the stroke and the coma, I had been busy, or at least ostensibly preoccupied, learning to drive, doing some lawyering, making some household changes, and otherwise. In any event, admitting some episodes of keen emotion, I had been constrained from tears.

Why? My reputed stoicism? Perchance. More likely that than a macho hang-up. Yet I have already excused myself from that allegation. I am no stoic; rather, I am very patient. And I know myself to be extraordinarily passionate. I know *that* in my bones as much as in my viscera, but, chiefly, I know *that* in my mind. I know it as the truth that I am the most passionate human being I have ever encountered.

If my tears were yet constrained it probably meant that my grief was still immature.

Meanwhile, an invitation had reached me from Ohio to speak in Columbus at the Pastors' Convocation annually sponsored by the Ohio Council of Churches. The date proposed was January 27, 1981. If I accepted this, I would either be traveling most of the next day, the anniversary date of Anthony's death, or I would be somewhere away from Block Island. I could not abide the notion of squandering that day in the hassles of travel—I had had enough of that in 1980 getting from Ontario to Rhode Island—so I decided I would go to Columbus, but pause, enroute home from Columbus, in New York City to spend January 28th there. It was appropriate. After all, Anthony and I had each spent much of our lives in the city, we both loved the city, and we had begun our collaboration as writers there. We had many, many friends in New York. Still, I knew when I decided to spend this particular day in the city that I would do so alone.

I went to Ohio and fulfilled the engagement on January 27th. Afterwards, I flew to New York, arriving in Manhattan in the early evening. I made one telephone call before retiring. I called the Rev. Thomas Pike, Rector of Calvary Church at Gramercy Park. Tom had been a good friend and sometime pastor to Anthony, to me, and to us, especially while I was ill. I asked Tom to commend Anthony at the eucharist he would celebrate the next day at Calvary Church.

the freedom of the dead

Any season of grieving is riddled with temptations to render death an idol, and though these may sometimes be bizarre, they are as often subtle. The subject is tender and attended by an etiquette that discourages candor. Other people, intending to be considerate of the bereaved, or supposing that they are easing the burden of a survivor, readily, if unwittingly, abet delusion.

I have already alluded to the common temptation to follow the dead into death either by deliberately and directly committing suicide, or, perhaps more often, by resigning from living, and instead of making the effort to continue to live, indulging some fantasy of the past or spending the remainder of one's time literally awaiting death. In such circumstances, the death that has happened works an estoppel of the life of one who survives.

Succumbing to such resignation is, I observe, accentuated significantly in situations of mandatory retirement at a specified age, regardless of health or capability for work, which have become routine in the American economy. The connotation of retirement institutionalized in this manner is that of waiting for death. The moral implication of such retirements is that a person is no longer useful or worthwhile in society and is, withal, officially discarded. So the outcast, having been pronounced as good as dead, waits to die to ratify his or her status as dead, by filling the time with passive diversions, practicing boredom, and dwelling in apprehension of death. The only thing that makes such an existence bearable, for multitudes, is the companionship of a spouse, but then it seems a further indignity should the couple not die simultaneously.

There are more temptations in grief, and many variations of each.

One of the most commonplace, I think, and one with which I had to struggle following Anthony's death, was the temptation to keep everything as it had apparently been, to freeze time by ritualizing the routine of household that had prevailed before his death. I know of neighbors on the Island who have been bereaved who keep the clothing and similar personal items, or the personal space, of the dead just so, as if in readiness for an imminent return of the dead. It is a morbid fantasy and a pagan practice, and to oppose it and eschew any hint of it, I promptly removed almost all of Anthony's personal possessions from the house, giving them away or discarding them.

I realized there was a special problem in the bedroom

where Anthony had slept, because Pollyanna, our eldest dog, a pensive creature, as she has always seemed to me, was long accustomed to waiting there each evening for Anthony to retire. Then, when he would come, he and the dog would play awhile. Anthony would talk at length to Pollyanna—usually highly literate comments (not baby talk like some people inflict upon their pets)—as if she understood it all. I have no reason to doubt that she did.

When Anthony was taken to the hospital by the rescue squad, Pollyanna went to that room and began her solitary vigil on his bed. And, when he did not return from the hospital, she, neither bashful nor stoic, would softly cry each day when the hour came when ordinarily Anthony would have been expected. Pollyanna would soon become utterly disconsolate if this went on indefinitely, and so Anthony's bed was taken away and the room's appearance changed. Pollyanna no longer pines, but she and I both know she is still waiting.

In short, it was important to *promptly* acknowledge the fact of Anthony's death—even for the dogs and the cat—not only verbally but, so to say, liturgically, by enacting the acknowledgment, for example, by altering the appearance of the household.

The Manger posed a similar question. The next time I went there, after having found Anthony's obituary on his desk, was some days later. Someone who had stopped by to offer me her condolences, asked to see Anthony's study. I showed the visitor the Manger, but, as I did so, I was conscious that if I kept it as Anthony had left it, it would soon become some sort of shrine, sentimental, vulgar, and profane. The next day I began to dismantle the place. I had collected, over the years, a considerable quantity and variety of circus memorabilia, so I decided the Manger would become the circus library.

Anthony and I had shared a reciprocity in the practical

regimen of the household at *Eschaton*. To a remarkable extent the division of responsibility between us coincided with our various capabilities or interests, and the efforts of each of us generally complemented those of the other. We did not expend much energy organizing *Eschaton*, that was a casual and spontaneous matter. This meant, however, that when Anthony died there was a gap in the rhythm of the household. For a time, I was tempted to try to fill that gap myself, until I faced the truth that much of what Anthony had done I was physically or otherwise incapable of doing. Besides, to try to substitute for Anthony's absence or to gainsay, somehow, that there was a void concealed the familiar temptation to pretend that nothing had changed. In fact, there had been a momentous change, and facing that reality was essential to creating a new mode of living in the household compatible with my own capabilities and congenial to my own priorities. *Eschaton* had been, while Anthony and I had lived together there, for ourselves and, I think, for many others from the Island and from the mainland, a blessed and hospitable place, but that did not make it sacrosanct.

As one might expect, there were friends who, upon Anthony's death, began to suggest that the answer for the practical problems of conducting and maintaining *Eschaton* as a household would be for me to locate some surrogate for Anthony, someone to assume the role that (it was erroneously presumed) he had played in my life and incidentally furnish me with greater freedom to write and mobility to travel for lectures and similar engagements on the mainland. Their logic usually featured admonitions about how precarious and unpredictable my health is and how, living alone, I risked another stroke or diabetic coma or other jeopardy and might not be able to summon help by my own effort. This argument typically posed the prospect of my being inadvertently discovered, after some time of helplessness and futility, dead. The same basic proposal was commended to me, by different friends, in several versions, variously casting as surrogate a secretary, a paramour, a houseboy, a bride.

I am not the sort to foreclose options quickly, and if I have any virtue, I suppose it to be open-mindedness. I listened attentively to such suggestions and appreciated the concern that prompted them. Perhaps someday, somewhere, I will have a wife, a houseboy, a paramour, or even a secretary (or all of them at once), but in the midst of both grief and mourning I yearned, more than anything else, to be alone, to return to myself, so to speak, to conserve myself for awhile, and to be freed of entanglements. I needed no surrogate for Anthony. That was very clear to me. And if I sought such a surrogate in another person it would be an imposition on that person as well as trivialize the good community which Anthony and I shared.

In that connection, the whole idea of a surrogate for the dead is an instance of the morbidness that seeks, in death, to cling to the past, maintain things as they were, and indulge the pretense that the dead are not quite dead.

Furthermore, speaking of my eccentric health, what my health required above all else, in the months following upon Anthony's death, was simply acceptance of the truth of his death. If that happened, as I have said before, I had no skepticism that an apropos style of living by myself would gradually, spontaneously emerge. After that, there would be leisure to cope with the further vulnerability of my life to other human beings.

In the autumn of 1980, there was a curious interlude in my grieving while I was in New York City for a few days

to consult a physician. During the experience the
temptation to retreat into the past in pretense that
Anthony was not dead and the idea of locating some
surrogate for Anthony merged, as it were. I had
remained in the city for a couple of days after seeing the
doctor, intending to shop and go to the theatre, and
perhaps also attend a movie and get a haircut—these
amenities being unavailable on the Island. Instead, I
found myself wandering about the city one afternoon. I
realized that I was not wandering aimlessly, but very
puposefully. I was expecting to see someone. In truth, I
was searching for Anthony. I had returned to where we
had first seen each other. I was retracing steps I had
originally walked seventeen years earlier. I kept expecting to sight Anthony among the passersby, though I had
no idea what I would do if I did see him. When I
understood whom I was looking for, the search was
exhausted, and this awful temptation fled from me. I
have been free of it ever since.

These matters I have here touched upon are not casual
or insignificant; they are similar, I think, to those
afflicting anyone seriously bereaved. What is involved in
such issues, in the end, is learning to respect the freedom
of the dead to be dead; honoring the dead in their status
as dead people, and refraining from harassment of the
dead by refusing to mythologize the dead or enshrine
them. What is at stake is recognition by those in grief of
the right of the dead to be regarded mortally, which is to
say, to be treated humanly in death.

a "medicine man"

The physician whom I saw in the city was a doctor Dan
Berrigan had urged me repeatedly to see, especially after
the medical misfortunes I had suffered during the
spring and summer. Berrigan had been plagued for

years by a chronic back problem, and this doctor had helped him; his professional credentials are those of a chiropractor, a biochemist, and a nutritionist. I learned that he has conviction about the healing capabilities of appropriate nutrition and a corresponding skepticism about the use and overuse of chemicals to effect symptomatic relief. His attitude is even more skeptical toward first resort to surgery and too-quick reliance upon mechanical devices. In short, his approach to healing challenges basic presuppositions—including those ethical—of commercialized medicine. Not surprisingly, he had endured spasmodic professional persecution because of it.

The circumstance that I went to him on Dan's commendation did not, I think, prejudice me about him one way or the other. After the laser fiasco, the stroke, and the needless coma, I was wary of anyone's touching me or treating me. I was, if anything, most inclined to muddle along on my own, improvising with my own health. That might not diminish the harm that could come to me, but on the whole, it seemed to me unlikely to increase it either.

I was impressed with the doctor's thoroughness. He is a holistic physician, but this is neither a fad nor a cult with him. He had insisted on auditing my medical records—which are, unfortunately, prodigious. It was soon evident, in our initial interview, that he had indeed read them carefully. He had also learned quite a bit about me as a person, in addition to information strictly pertinent to me as a patient. At Dan's suggestion he had also read *A Second Birthday,* and therefore knew of my understanding of pain and suffering, health and healing, death and dying. So he was knowledgeable, both objectively and subjectively, about me. His examination of me was as thorough as I have ever had and notable for the minimum of gadgets and contraptions he engaged.

Since my most serious immediate health issue has to do with blood circulation, he has designed a regimen of nutrients, compounded from natural substances and minerals, which I have been consuming, along with following the dietary scheme I have lived by since the crisis in my health in 1968. As I write this, I have observed this routine conscientiously for nearly ten months. Within that time, though I tire sometimes of organizing so many pills and capsules to take, there has been an astonishing improvement in the circulation in my legs. Nurse Donnelly calls it "startling." It is. Where there has been atrophy, there is now feeling—heat or cold, pinprick or tickle, pain or pleasure—I can feel any one of them in my legs now, and I can distinguish each from the others. Before, I could feel nothing—nothing at all. Where there has been discoloration—my legs had turned ashen—now a normal color has been restored. Where there has been calloused skin, now viable tissue has returned.

I remain so chastened about my own health that I venture no predictions, and very few conclusions, from this most recent experience. I have, manifestly, for the time being, been spared the kind of surgery that had been advocated while I was prey at that hospital in New London. And, I can say I respect enormously the common sense of the doctor to whom Dan brought me. What he affirms about the healing capabilities of conscientious nutrition—a matter notoriously neglected or suppressed by commercialized medicine for transparently obvious reasons—makes theological sense to me, too. A miracle in healing is not the conjuring of some magic, nor a disruption of the created order, or something supernatural. Rather, healing exemplifies the redemption of fallen Creation, the restoration of the created order, the return to the usual, the normative, the natural.

a lawyer's work

If politics, from time to time, has spawned for me prosaic temptation to mistake career for vocation, being a lawyer has not bothered me in any comparable way. I was spared that before I even entered Harvard Law School because of my disposition of the substantive issue of career versus vocation while I was a graduate fellow at the London School of Economics and Political Science. As I have remarked heretofore, I had elected then to pursue *no* career. To put it theologically, I died to the idea of career and to the whole typical array of mundane calculations, grandiose goals and appropriate schemes to reach them. I renounced, simultaneously, the embellishments—like money, power, success—associated with careers in American culture, along with the ethics requisite to obtaining such condiments. I do not say this haughtily; this was an aspect of my conversion to the gospel so, in fact, I say it humbly.

In the time that intervened between London and Harvard (part of which I spent traveling extensively in Europe and in Asia—often at the behest of the World Student Christian Federation—and the remainder of which I served in the Second Armored Division—*Hell-on-Wheels,* was its watchword—assigned to the North Atlantic Treaty Organization forces) my renunciation of ambition in favor of vocation became resolute; I suppose some would think, eccentric. When I began law studies, I consider that I had few, if any, romantic illusions about becoming a lawyer and I most certainly did not indulge any fantasies that God had called me, by some specific instruction, to be an attorney, or for that matter, to be a

member of any profession or any occupation. I had come
to understand the meaning of vocation more simply and
quite differently.

I believed then, as I do now, that I am called in the
Word of God—as is *everyone* else—to the vocation of
being human, nothing more and nothing less. I
confessed then, as I do now, that to be a Christian means
to be called to be an exemplary human being. And, to be
a Christian *categorically* does not mean being religious.
Indeed, all religious versions of the gospel are profani-
ties. Within the scope of the calling to be merely, but
truly, human, any work, including that of any profession,
can be rendered a sacrament of that vocation. On the
other hand, no profession, discipline or employment, as
such, is a vocation.

Law students, along with those in medicine, engi-
neering, architecture, the military, among others, are
subjected to indoctrinations, the effort of such being to
make the students conform quickly and thoroughly to
that prevailing stereotype deemed most beneficial to the
profession and to its survival as an institution, its
influence in society, and its general prosperity. At the
Harvard Law School, this process is heavy, intensive, and
unrelenting, though I imagine that such indoctrinations
are all the more so in pseudo-professional institutions,
like those training insurance agents, stockbrokers, or
realtors. Over and over again, while I was in the law
school, I was astonished at how eagerly many of my peers
surrendered to this regimen of professionalistic conditioning, often squelching their own most intelligent
opinions or creative impulses in order to conform or to
appear to be conforming.

Initiation into the legal profession, as it is played out at
a place like the Harvard Law School, is, as one would
expect, elaborately mythologized, asserts an aura of

tradition, and retains a reputation for civility. All of these insinuate that this process is benign, though, both empirically and in principle, it is demonic. One notices that the medical establishment has gone much further than has the legal profession in indulging this sort of mythologizing, with the conspicuous collaboration of commercial television, and, before that, the movies. (After all, the mythological forerunner of *Marcus Welby* was *Dr. Christian*.) I think none of the other professions has countenanced such pretentious and gratuitous self-images as the medical profession has, but the same issue of mythologizing is associated with all the professions, and with most other occupations as well. There is radical discrepancy between myth and truth in internal indoctrinations focused on conforming practitioners and external publicity propagated about the various professions.

I understand in hindsight that the vocational attitude I had formed in London, and later, the experience I had as law student, apprehended the legal profession specifically, and the professions, disciplines and occupations in general, in their status among the fallen principalities and powers engaged (regardless of apparently benign guises and pretenses) in coercing, stifling, captivating, intimidating, and otherwise victimizing human beings. The demand for conformity in a profession commonly signifies a threat of death.

In that connection, my commitment to vocation instead of career began, while I was still in the law school, to sponsor far-reaching implications for how I could spend the rest of my life. Anyway, I suffered the overkill ethos of the Harvard Law School—I think—with enough poise as a human being to quietly, patiently, vigilantly resist becoming conformed to this world.

The upshot of that resistance was that I emerged from

the law school as someone virtually opposite of what a Harvard Law School graduate is projected by the prevailing system to be. I do say *that* proudly, and gladly.

Do not misunderstand me: I enjoyed the law school, but I did not take it with the literally dead earnestness of those of my peers who had great careers at stake. I respected the intellectual vigor of its environment, but I was appalled by the overwhelming subservience of legal education to the commercial powers and the principalities of property. I thought that a law school should devote at least as much attention in its curriculum to the rights and causes of people as it does to vested property interests of one kind or another. I also thought, while I was in law school, that *justice* is a suitable topic for consideration in practically every course or specialization. Alas, it was seldom mentioned, and the term itself evoked ridicule, as if justice were a subject beneath the sophistication of lawyers.

Since 1956, when I was graduated, I have been enabled to remain in touch with legal education in a more than perfunctory manner because I am often invited as a visiting lecturer in various law schools around the country. Thus I am aware that there have been some significant, if modest, curricular reforms in many law schools lately, including work in urban law, poverty law, consumer law, and some cross-disciplinary efforts between law and other graduate disciplines.

Be that as it may, when I went to the East Harlem ghetto directly upon finishing at the law school, and began to practice law there on my own, it was regarded by most of my peers as a curious venture, idiosyncratic and controversial. *My People Is the Enemy* tells of that experience. That book had some impact in exposing the neglect of people, especially the dispossessed of the inner city regions, by the legal profession, in part attributable to the co-option of lawyers and legal education by commercial or similar principalities and powers. For instance, while Robert Kennedy was Attorney General of the United States, an emissary of Kennedy's came to me one day in New York City. He announced that the Attorney General had determined to convene a conference of lawyers from areas throughout the nation to examine issues of the law and the poor, and to consider how the legal profession might more responsibly serve the needs and interests of the poor in society. The Attorney General, my informant declared, had read *My People Is the Enemy* and had been moved by it, and had dispatched him, he stated, "to pick your brain" about these matters in the hope that this would yield ideas for the conference which was contemplated. "I had better tell you first, however," my visitor confided, "that you will not be invited to speak to the conference . . . you're too radical." I found such candor appealing, and the interview commenced.

Robert Kennedy was, however, mistaken in an assessment that, as a lawyer, I am "radical." I do not think such labels—"radical," "liberal," "conservative," "reactionary"—edifying because they are so ambivalent in meaning, and I infrequently use them myself. But, if such classifications are invoked, in my opinion I could scarcely be counted as "radical" within the context of the legal tradition that has been inherited in America. My practice of law for a quarter of a century amply verifies this. I have been an advocate for the poor, for the urban underclass, for freedom riders and war resisters, for people deprived of elementary rights: children, women, blacks, Hispanics, native Americans, political prisoners, homosexuals, the elderly, the handicapped, clergy accused of heresy, women aspiring to priesthood. The consistent concerns of my practice have been the values of the constitutional system, due process of law, and the rule of law. What is radical about that? Perhaps these represent views of the law and society that could have been said to be radical in the thirteenth century, at the time the Magna Charta was ratified, but if they seem radical nowadays it is because so few lawyers care about them.

In East Harlem, on Block Island, in ecclesiastical courts as well as secular venues, as in the law school, I simply do not share in that feigned professional sophistication that sponsors and inculcates the indifference of lawyers to the constitutional priorities, particularly the Bill of Rights, or that rationalizes a preference for the *laissez faire* interests of commerce as opposed to the freedom, safety, and welfare of human beings, or that asserts a so-called sanctity of property that devalues and demeans human life.

Despite the notoriety that has been attached to the witness of civil disobedience, notably in the era of Martin Luther King, Jr., and then in the antiwar movement of the Sixties, there has been little threat to the rule of law in these protests. In fact, the major burden of them has been to act to redeem the constitutional system. The substantive danger to this society, so far as law is concerned, comes from the operation of lawless authority and the substitution of the power of coercion for the rule of law. For more than two decades now, the nation has suffered one outrageous spasm of official lawlessness after another. If this came into climactic focus in Watergate, in the aborted impeachment of President Nixon, and the nominal punishment of a handful of culprits in high places, that comes nowhere near exhausting the scandal of illegal, unconstitutional, and often criminal offenses accomplished by military, police, security, and intelligence officials within the federal regime, not to mention their counterparts in state and some local agencies. Reread the Kerner Commission findings. Recall the literally fantastic machinations of successive C.I.A. administrations, and then notice as well that the C.I.A. and the rest of the so-called intelligence complex still operates without presidential restraint, without parliamentary control, without any effectual accountability under the American constitutional system. Meanwhile, the F.B.I. is extolled by the incumbent President for its past flagrant infractions of constitutional limitations; and an immense and intricate scheme to rehabilitate its public image, following upon the most constitutionally obnoxious disclosures of official lawlessness under the auspices of J. Edgar Hoover, has been mounted, which involves the official procurement of crime. At the same time, the police power in most state and urban jurisdictions has been transmuted—partly under the patronage of the Pentagon—from a civilian to a paramilitary force in society, reflecting a contempt for constitutional safeguards and an overkill reliance upon violence. And all of this, and much, much more of the same, has been accompanied by the unrelenting barrage of propaganda on commercial television glorifying official violence as heroic, requisite, and efficient, even though it usurps constitutional rule.

advocacy as a pastoral gift

When I first arrived in 1956 in East Harlem, I supposed that the rudimentary problem respecting the law was a failure to fully implement the existing American legal system among citizens who were economically dispossessed and who were victimized by racism. My supposition was, I soon enough discovered, mistaken. The issue, so far as the law was concerned, in the ghetto was the existence of another ruling system, distinct and apart from the constitutional and legal system pertaining elsewhere in the nation, based on coercion and the threat of coercion by those institutions and people who had commandeered the capabilities of coercion. It was a system of lawless authority, of official violence, a primitive substitution for the law. I wrote then that if such an extraordinary condition were allowed to continue and to fester, it would, sooner or later, infect and afflict the whole of this society. It has. There is a connection—direct and terrible and coherent—between the kind of regime to be found in the ghettoes in the Fifties and the way lawless authority and official violence dominate the life of most of this society today. And let no one pretend that a place like Block Island has been exempt from similar issues: until only some few years ago contempt for due process of law was the most conspicuous attribute of the town's administration.

If I hold lawyers especially responsible for the usurpation of constitutional rule in America because they, as a class and a profession, have been so lured and preoccupied with greed and apathy, I also ask myself, nearly every morning, whether my remaining an attorney condones—or appears to condone—the decadence against which I complain. Anthony and I often talked of this relentless tension that I feel in being a lawyer. Without his care and wisdom—sometimes delivered somberly, sometimes in repartée—that tension, I am aware, heightens. I do not know, now, what the limits of my endurance in the circumstances are. I am certain, however, that stoicism can be of no relevance.

A critical dimension of this tension occasioned by being a biblical person who works as a lawyer is that the role of legal advocate at once coincides with and interferes with the pastoral calling to which I am disposed charismatically. In that calling, advocacy expresses the freedom in Christ to undertake the cause of another—including causes deemed "hopeless," to intercede for the need of another—without evaluating it, but just because the need is apparent, to become vulnerable—even unto death—in the place of another. By contrast, advocacy in the law is contained within the bounds of the adversary system, with all its implications of competitiveness, aggression, facetious games, debater's craft, and winning *per se*. There have been circumstances in my experience when the advocacy of the Christian in the world coincides with the advocacy of the lawyer (as in the cases concerning the ordination of women), but there seem to be far more instances when the one interferes with the other (as in war resister cases). In part, here, of course, I am pleading within the legal profession for a more holistic approach to clients and cases than that afforded by the adversary system. Yet, more than that, I continue to be haunted with the ironic impression that I may have to renounce being a lawyer the better to be an advocate.

reprise

Over and over again, in the months ensuing the death of Anthony, I have been intrigued by the redundancy of history—my personal history, but also history in a more generalized sense. I do not imply that I thought history was repeating itself in some mindless, automatic way, but rather that the death provoked my memory, as it did for others, and my recall in both grief and mourning was so vivid that an event or experience from the past took on new prominence in the present, sometimes overshadowing or even preempting whatever was happening at the moment. This has to do with the mystery of time that I have mentioned previously, and with the dialectic of time into which biblical people enter so that they are simultaneously living in the moment and in eternity, or within the realm of time but outside of time. Or, as I have sometimes put the same idea, both the Apocalypse and the Eschaton impinge upon *every* moment.

This was the frame of mind (or should I say, to use the jargon, "the time frame") in which I received the news of the witness of the Plowshares Eight. Of course I recalled especially the Catonsville Nine, but mainly I was reminded of the reports in the Book of the Acts of the Apostles (Acts 3:1–4:22; 5:17-42; 6:8-15; 7:54–8:3, etc.).

Dorothy Day, of blessed memory, did not like to be called (as she often was, for good reason) a saint, because it usually meant that she was not being taken seriously. She heard it as an accusation—a device ostensibly distinguishing her from ordinary people so as to simultaneously discount her words and deeds while exempting others from moral responsibility to speak out and act.

The Berrigan brothers have shared a similar burden since the time of the Catonsville Nine action in the spring of 1968, though they most commonly are accused of being prophets. It is a version of the same device. Lately it has had currency in connection with the trial of the Plowshares Eight in the Montgomery County Court, near Philadelphia. Six other people, along with Daniel and Philip, have been convicted of entering a General Electric plant, where they dented two nuclear warhead nose cones for the Mark 12A first-strike nuclear weapons, and spilled some blood on official papers.

At the scene of the trial, as well as elsewhere during the event, opinion was virtually unanimous, as far as I could tell, that the effort of the Berrigans and the Plowshares compatriots had been characteristically prophetic. I heard that assessment from a wide and diverse array of clergy and laity, including a few bishops, from assorted alumni of the Vietnam resistance, from academic professionals and students, as well as from neighbors and friends. The same conclusion was evident in the exasperation displayed in the prosecutor's attitude, in the sympathies of some of the press, and even through the incredible density and insecurity evinced by the judge throughout the proceedings.

The jeopardy for the Plowshares Eight—some have been sentenced to as much as three to ten years in prison—is such that their action cannot be classified as a prank and put aside. At the same time, I gather that it is difficult for many citizens to imagine that such an act could have a decisive impact on public policy and alter America's overdependence on overkill nuclear capability or diminish the prospect of nuclear apocalypse in the immediate future. The truth is it is practically impossible for most Americans to contemplate *any* action that could change the probabilities of nuclear catastrophe: most Americans have become fatalistic about the arms race, and most see nothing that they could do *without significant risk to themselves,* comparable to the jeopardy of the Plowshares Eight, that would influence the penultimate outcome of the arms race. Most Americans have resigned to cynicism, despair, quietism. Thus, when the Berrigans turn up again in court, having performed a liturgical act to exorcise the hosts of death rampant in the Pentagon and in the American war commerce, it seems incongruous, disproportionate to their jeopardy, foolish, and a nuisance to the authorities. The simplest way to deal with the Berrigan witness—apart from ignoring it altogether—is to dismiss it as "prophetic." Then conscience becomes narrowed in its meaning to idiosyncracy, rather than being a reality definitively human, and everyone who is not a prophet seems exempted from either possessing a conscience or exercising it.

This sophistry is sometimes embellished by the allegation that the Berrigans are *radical*. That is, of course, usually an empty term used like a curse to incite, rather than to edify or identify. Sometimes it does have an ideological connotation, but, as anyone attentive to the Berrigan literature has learned, it has nothing of that if applied to them, since they have no ideological stance. (*No* Christian does.) Moreover, legally, in the Plowshares trial, the Berrigans and the other defendants could not fairly be deemed radical, since their rationale for their conduct stood well within the doctrine of justification for civil disobedience in both the law of the jurisdiction, Pennsylvania, and that of higher authority: that is, the Nuremburg principle. In protesting the nuclear weapons commerce and in interceding for a human destiny, the Berrigan brothers and their peers were theologically no more "radical" than was the Pope when he visited Hiroshima, just as the Plowshares trial got underway, to exhort everyone to oppose the arms race.

There are those who suppose that the action of the Plowshares Eight represents an indulgence in nostalgia, a yearning to reconstitute the resistance of the Sixties around the nuclear issue and to replay the earlier tumult. I have never found the Berrigans fascinated by any such romantic nonsense. Quite the contrary, what they say about the nuclear threat to humanity sounds to me grave, sober, realistic, and literally ominous. Furthermore, the tactics of the Berrigan witness do not appear to me to be either inept or inapt, for all that some may see them as esoteric or absurd. In the Plowshares action, as at Catonsville, and in actions between those two, the Berrigans, as I understand the matter, have been celebrating liturgies that expose and rebuke the power of death in our midst and proclaim the efficacy of the resurrection from death. In Christian terms, both the witness and the tactics of the witness have been most traditional and commonplace.

If either public or personal responses to the Berrigan witness are not to be some form of cop-out, the rubric for comprehending what they are saying and doing is supplied, manifestly, by the Book of the Acts of the Apostles. Acts is the chronicle of the many arrests, trials, imprisonments, exiles, tortures, and executions suffered by the pioneer Christians at the behest of the ruling authorities. In those confrontations, the issue is not whether the apostles in their witness are "effective," or otherwise have prospects of what the world knows as "success" or "victory." The issue, instead, is whether the apostles speak and act faithfully in the gospel, and thus exemplify in their living the truth and power of the Word of God transcending and disrupting the reign of death, and the idolatry of the power of death, in any and all regimes of this world.

Don't ask me whether the Berrigans can be said to be prophets. For the time being that is irrelevant, anyway. We, and they, will find out about that in the leisure of the Eschaton. For now, I regard them simply as Christians, standing squarely within the Apostolic precedent, engaged in a witness both venerable and normative, bespeaking the resurrection of Jesus.

a view of afterdeath

Some people, I suppose, would consider it virtually obligatory—in a book concerned with death, grief, and mourning—to speculate about the afterlife, so called. I will, literally, not do so here. The term itself is (at the least) a misnomer. More often than not, "afterlife" refers to a mush of vain and pagan imaginings.

The real issue is, anyway, not "afterlife" but "after-death." Any bereaved person, or anyone contemplating his or her own death, is likely to give some thought to what, if anything, happens experientially when a person dies. One reason such brooding is commonly incoherent or merely self-serving is that it presupposes the linear reality of time and does not probe the mystery of time, especially the relation of time to the bondage to death in the present age, in the era of the Fall, or the disruption of time and the emancipation from time that is implicated in conversion, as I have previously discussed.

The most radical confusion about afterdeath, however, has to do with the transliteration of the resurrection as some idea of immortality. This is an interpolation frequently attributable to preachers, and it is categorically false. Anyone who has read some of my work will be familiar with the significance I attach to distinguishing resurrection from immortality. In my view, immortality, essentially, is no more than an elaborate synonym for remembrance of the dead, though there are attached to it multifarious notions of spiritual and/or material survival of death. Resurrection, however, refers to the transcendence of the power of death, and of the fear or thrall of the power of death, here and now, in this life, in this world. Resurrection, thus, has to do with life, and indeed, the fulfillment of life, *before* death.

I am aware that some may cite my own experience in coma at that hospital in New London as if it has evidentiary significance for the idea of an afterlife. I do not. I consider that the experience warrants no such inflated inference. What happened then, so far as I understand it, was an ordinary near death episode. It may offer some insight into death as an empirical reality, it betells nothing thereafter.

For all I know there may be, in some sense, personal survival after death, but that is not what the resurrection is, *in esse,* concerned with. Where confusion reigns and the distinction between resurrection and immortality is lost or suppressed, it is common to find people, frantic in their embrace of one or another versions of survival after death, rejecting life in this world, including, typically, the gift of their own lives. That is more than an escapist doctrine, feigning to justify withdrawal, default, or cowardice so far as life in this world is concerned; it issues in idolatry of death. And its denial of the efficacy of the resurrection of Jesus Christ is tantamount to blasphemy.

These imaginations about personal survival provoke a plethora of other questions when they are associated with reputed communications between the living and the dead. I strive to remain open-minded, and I think I have great appreciation for the intuitive realm, but the fact remains that so-called paranormal (another misnomer; if this is part of reality, the appropriate word is *normal*) experience has been, at least in American culture, so preempted and promoted by quacks, cultists, charlatans, and others exploiting the guilt inherent in grief for profit or notoriety, that intelligent opinion about the subject is practically precluded. Anthony and I exhaustively researched, for instance, the alleged communications, through assorted mediums, of Bishop Pike with his son Jim, who was thought to have committed suicide. The product of those researches is included in our biography, *The Death and Life of Bishop Pike*. We concluded that our friend, the Bishop, had been cruelly importuned, though that view is quite inconclusive as to the merits of the question of whether there can be credible communication betwixt the living and the dead.

Whatever the disposition of that question, it represents a trivial aspect of afterdeath. Biblical faith promises the consummation of *all* created life, in all its range and diversity, in the end and fullness of time, and it offers images, pictures, parables, and stories characterizing that consummation (e.g., Revelation 21). There is no timetable, there are no literal descriptions, the biblical witness is no horoscope of the Kingdom. The veracity of the promise, thus, is not dependent upon prooftexts, predictions, or tests of God like those conducted in seances or similar demonstrations, but upon the witness of the risen life in this history in this world, as the Church, where the Church is faithful, and as the Communion of Saints.

I am so persuaded that the resurrection means the accessibility, for human beings, on behalf of all of life, of the power of the Word of God, which the whole of Creation enjoys in being made, overcoming the power of death here and now, that I expect the consummation eagerly. Anthony shared this piety with me. That is why our common occupation became the work of prayer. When Anthony died, it did not occur to me to somehow seek explicit communication with the dead. (I doubt that would have been grief therapy for me.)

Instead, my mourning is the answer to my grieving. I rejoice that Anthony lived, while he lived, and that when he died he had *already* known the resurrection from the dead.

Once upon a time, while Anthony Towne and I were immigrating to Block Island, a friend from New York joined the two of us in moving stuff by car and ferry from the city to the Island. We arrived in Old Harbor on a gray and dismal November day and disembarked. Our friend looked all around, surveying the boarded-up shops and desolate hotels and the somewhat scruffy characters loitering around the pier. "God!" he cried with anguish, "this is the end of the world!" "No," I responded, "it is the beginning of the world!"

That evening there was a long discussion at dinner

amongst the three of us about what to name the house and premises where we were to live on the Island. We disdained names such as "Sea Breeze" or "Foggy Bottom." At last Anthony recalled the exchange of words when we had arrived on the ferry and proposed that we name our place *Eschaton,* because *eschaton* means the end of the world coinciding with the beginning of the world as the Kingdom of God. Thus, in common usage, *eschaton* means hope.

At *Eschaton,* Anthony and I lived in the simplicity of that consummate hope.

a eucharist at Calvary

It was January 28, 1981, the nominal anniversary of Anthony's death.

I would spend the day alone in the city, as I had decided, until six-thirty in the evening, when the eucharist was to be celebrated at Calvary Church with, as it is often styled, "special intention" for Anthony Towne.

I do not know much more than that about the day. My recall is as surrealistic and impressionistic, as eerie and intense as the corresponding day a year earlier had been, when I traveled from Ontario to Anthony's deathbed.

I did walk a lot. Commonly, if I walk much, the exertion occasions pain. I walked a great distance that day oblivious to pain.

I walked for blocks in East Harlem, my beloved old neighborhood. It was the place in the city where I had first felt accepted and at home.

I walked in Greenwich Village; I found the building from which Anthony had been evicted. I rejoiced quietly in my failure in stopping that eviction.

I went again to West Seventy-ninth Street, where we had shared a household and had begun to practice hospitality.

I stood outside and looked upon Columbia-Presbyterian Hospital. In there Anthony had waited twelve hours while I was in surgery. It was where I was supposed to die but didn't.

I walked.

I walked some more.

I walked the city that day.

But, this time, I was not searching for the dead. I knew I would not glimpse Anthony no matter where I went. So, mainly, all that day, I wept. I wailed. I gnashed teeth.

And then, suddenly, it seemed I was walking down an aisle. I could recognize the interior of Calvary Church. Only the chancel was lighted, just the immediate vicinity of the altar.

I sat down somewhere in the dimness of the nave.

I picked up a prayerbook and opened it.

After a time, a figure approached me. It was Tom Pike. He embraced me, gingerly, as if he knew that I might shatter if his touch were too robust. He invited me to join him and a few parishioners who were gathered near the altar.

The service began.

At the time of the offertory, when the bread and wine were placed upon the altar, Tom spoke gently of Anthony. A prayer was said. The meal was blessed, the bread was broken and eaten, the cup was passed, *this* eucharist was celebrated.

All the while, I had been holding the open prayerbook. I looked down at it. It was opened at the Service for the Burial of the Dead.

By now my tears were done.

POEM

(for Katherine Breydert)

POEM
is a shape
of words each of
which must be where it
is the way geese in solitary
flight concatenate an argument for
solipsistic poetry—I refer, of course,
to T. S. Eliot and the objective correlative—
and at the apogee a convex of elegant honks suggests
(geese know more than poets do about survival)
that the epiphenomenon of communications
is a serendipity fugitive migrants
ought to cherish or revel in
as words merrily revel
in the flight of
a solitary
POEM

ANTHONY TOWNE